# New Dramaturgies of Contemporary Opera

*New Dramaturgies of Contemporary Opera* is the first and only book that approaches the dramaturgy of contemporary opera from the unique perspectives of living practitioners (composers, librettists, directors, producers, singers, dramaturgs, and administrators) who provide valuable first-hand insight into the coming into being of an opera today.

The edited collection captures the ethos of contemporary opera-making in the global context and serves as a timely intervention in addressing the array of heterogenous dramaturgical practices that go into making an opera today in an era of flux. The collection is split into four parts: Part I presents the new dramaturgical considerations that the field is currently exploring; Part II investigates the ways in which non-Western cultures and perspectives can and have been represented; Part III explores the roles of space, nature, and environment in contemporary opera; and finally, Part IV looks at the ways in which technology has intersected with the creation of contemporary opera.

With perspectives from practitioners throughout, this collection is essential reading for advanced students, researchers, and scholars of contemporary opera, as well as practicing dramaturgs in this field.

**Jingyi Zhang** is a Ph.D. candidate in musicology at Harvard University. As a music and cultural historian, her research interests center on themes of racial identity, mobility, media technology, and decolonial thinking in 19th to 21st century songs, opera, and theater.

## Focus on Dramaturgy

Series Editor: Magda Romanska

The *Focus on Dramaturgy* series from Routledge - developed in collaboration with TheTheatreTimes.com – is devoted to the craft of dramaturgy from multiple contemporary perspectives. This groundbreaking comprehensive series is authored by top professionals in the field, addressing a variety of current hot topics in dramaturgy.

The series is edited by Magda Romanska, an author of the critically-acclaimed *Routledge Companion to Dramaturgy*, dramaturg, writer, theatre scholar, and Editor-in-Chief of TheTheatreTimes.com.

**Dramaturgy of Form**
Performing Verse in Contemporary Theatre
*Kasia Lech*

**The Dramaturgy of History**
*Tom Bryant*

**Dramaturgy of Sex on Stage in Contemporary Theatre**
*Edited by Kate Mulley*

**The Dramaturgy of Performing Science**
New Work in Interdisciplinary Contexts
*Jules Odendahl-James*

**New Dramaturgies of Contemporary Opera**
The Practitioners' Perspectives
*Edited by Jingyi Zhang*

For more information about this series, please visit: https://www.routledge.com/performance/series/RFOD

# New Dramaturgies of Contemporary Opera

## The Practitioners' Perspectives

**Edited by Jingyi Zhang**

Routledge
Taylor & Francis Group
LONDON AND NEW YORK

First published 2025
by Routledge
4 Park Square, Milton Park, Abingdon, Oxon OX14 4RN

and by Routledge
605 Third Avenue, New York, NY 10158

*Routledge is an imprint of the Taylor & Francis Group, an informa business*



*British Library Cataloguing-in-Publication Data*
A catalogue record for this book is available from the British Library

ISBN: 978-1-032-61157-0 (hbk)
ISBN: 978-1-032-61158-7 (pbk)
ISBN: 978-1-003-46228-6 (ebk)

DOI: 10.4324/9781003462286

Typeset in Times New Roman
by KnowledgeWorks Global Ltd.

# Contents

# About the Contributors

**Noa Frenkel** is a contralto and versatile artist with an affinity for many musical styles and an extensive vocal range. Her concert repertoire ranges from Renaissance to contemporary music. Recent concert appearances include Sofia Gubaidulina's *Hour of the Soul* at the Konzerthaus Vienna, Luigi Nono's opera *Al Gran Sole Carico D'Amore* at the Theater Basel, Berio's *Ofanim* with the ensemble Intercontemporain at the Festival d'Automne, Paris, a world premiere of Chaya Czernowin's opera *Heart Chamber* at the Deutsche Oper Berlin, Nono's *Guai ai Gelidi Mostry* at the Konzerthaus Wien and Salzburg Festival, Pascal Dusapin's opera *Penthesilea* at the Paris Philharmonie, and world premieres of Johannes Kalitzke's opera *Kapitän Nemos Bibliothek* at the Schwetzingen Festival SWR and the Bregenz Festival, and Thierry Pecou's *Until The Lions* at the Opera du Rhin, Strasbourg, and Czernowin's opera *Pnima* at the Staatstheater Darmstadt. Homepage: www.noafrenkel.com

**David T. Little** is a composer known for stage, concert, and screen works permeated with the power of the unexpected. A natural musical storyteller with "a knack for overturning musical conventions" (*The New York Times*), Little has drawn acclaim for his operas, including *Dog Days*, *JFK*, *Vinkensport*, or *The Finch Opera*, and the Grammy-nominated *Soldier Songs* and *Black Lodge.* He is currently developing a new work commissioned by the Metropolitan Opera/Lincoln Center Theater New Works Program. Published by Boosey & Hawkes, Little holds a Ph.D. from Princeton University and chairs the Composition program at the Mannes School of Music. Homepage: www.davidtlittle.com

**Beth Morrison** is a Grammy-nominated producer, recipient of the Musical America Award for Best Artist of the Year and Agent of Change, and a Kennedy Center Next50 Honoree. Hailed as a "contemporary opera mastermind" (*LA Times*) and "a powerhouse leading the industry to new heights" (*WQXR*), Morrison is an opera and theater producer, President and Creative Producer of Beth Morrison Projects, and Founding Co-Director of the PROTOTYPE Festival. She created Beth Morrison Projects (BMP) in 2006 to identify and support the work of emerging and established living composers, and to create a new kind of opera ("Beth Morrison is her own genre"—*Opera News*). BMP is celebrated as having been an industry disruptor and is now a tastemaker at the forefront of musical and theatrical innovation by commissioning, developing, producing, and touring the groundbreaking new works of a diverse group of living composers and their collaborators, which take the form of opera-theater, music-theater, and vocal-theater. Homepage: www.bethmorrisonprojects.org

**Jelena Novak** works as a principal researcher and assistant professor at CESEM, FCSH, and Universidade NOVA de Lisboa. Her fields of interest are modern and contemporary music, recent opera, singing and new media, capitalist realism, voice studies, and feminine identities in music. She explores these fields as a researcher, lecturer, writer, dramaturge, music critic, editor, and curator focused on bringing together critical theory and contemporary art. Her most recent books include *Postopera: Reinventing the Voice-Body* (2015), *Operofilia* (2018), and *Einstein on the Beach: Opera beyond Drama* (co-edited with John Richardson, 2019). Most recently, she collaborated as a dramaturge in the opera *Deca* in 17 songs (Children, 2022) by Irena Popović at the National Theatre in Belgrade. She is currently working on a book called *Opera in the Expanded Field*, which focuses on what it means and what it takes to sing beyond human.

**Ellen Pearlman** is a new media artist, curator, critic, and educator. A Visiting Research Scholar at NYU's Tandon School of Engineering and a Senior Research Assistant Professor at RISEBA University in Latvia, she was a Fulbright Research Scholar at the Department of Mathematics and Informatics at the University of Warsaw, Poland, a MIT Research Fellow, a two-time Fulbright Specialist in Art, New Media and Technology, a Vertigo STARTS Artist Laureate and a Zero1 American Arts Incubator/US State Department artist. She received her Ph.D. from the School of Creative Media, Hong Kong City University, where her Ph.D. thesis received Highest Global Honors from Leonardo LABS Abstracts.

**Krisztina Rosner** (Meiji University) is a Tokyo-based Hungarian researcher and practitioner of contemporary performing arts. Her Ph.D. thesis focuses on the actor's presence and the performative aspects of silence. Her current research focuses on transmedia and technology, with a special emphasis on the nonhuman aspects of contemporary Japanese performance. She is also active as an actor and director, and has given workshops in the United States, Japan, and Europe. She is the founder of the Tokyo Acting Class. Grants include the UNESCO-Aschberg Bursary for Performing Artists (2006), the "Eotvos" Hungarian State Research Grant (2008), the Hungarian Academy of Science Book Publication Grant (2011), then Japan Foundation Postdoctoral Research Fellowship (Hosei University, Tokyo, 2014), and the Japan Society for the Promotion of Science (Waseda University 2015–2017). Homepage: www.tinarosner.com

**Kelley Rourke** (librettist, dramaturg, and translator) has collaborated with composers John Glover, Laura Karpman, Wang Lu, Ben Moore, Kenji Oh, and Kamala Sankaram. She has created English adaptations of more than 20 existing works. Her work has been seen on the stages of the Metropolitan Opera, Washington National Opera, English National Opera, Royal Opera House Covent Garden, The Glimmerglass Festival, Chicago Opera Theater, Carnegie Hall, and Opera Parallèle, among many others. After serving as AOI's Librettist Mentor for three cycles, she was named Artistic Advisor in 2022. She holds degrees in Piano Performance and Arts Management. Homepage: www.kelleyrourke.com

**Kamala Sankaram** is called "one of the most exciting opera composers in the country" (*The Washington Post*) for moving between the worlds of experimental music and contemporary opera. As a biracial Indian American and sitarist, Sankaram has drawn on Indian classical music in many of her works, including *Thumbprint*, *A Rose*, *Monkey and Francine in the City of Tigers*, and *Jungle Book*. Also known for pushing the boundaries of form, she has created an opera for the trees of Prospect Park, a techno-noir featuring live data mining and a chorus of 25 singing tablet computers, and the world's first virtual reality opera. Homepage: www.kamalasankaram.com

**Ashley Kelly Tata** (*they/she*) directs multi-media works of theater, contemporary opera, performance, cyberformance, live music, and immersive experiences that have been presented in venues and festivals throughout the US and internationally. These works have been developed with residencies at BAM, Mercury Story, Coffey Street Studios, EMPAC, and with a Map Grant. Tata's collaborators have included the composers Kate Soper, Ted Hearne, David T. Little and Bora Yoon among others. Tata is currently a Visiting Assistant Professor of Theater & Performance at Bard College. Homepage: tatatime.live

**Du Yun**, born and raised in Shanghai, China, is a composer, performer, and performance artist, working at the intersection of orchestras, opera, chamber music, theater, cabaret, oral tradition, public performance, sound installation, electronics, and noise. Her last major opera, *Angel's Bone*, won a Pulitzer Prize for music in 2017; in 2018 she was named a Guggenheim Fellow; and in 2019 she was nominated for a Grammy Award. She was hailed by *The New York Times* as a groundbreaking artist and was listed by *The Washington Post* as one of the top 35 female composers. Known as chameleonic in her protean artistic outputs, her music is championed by some of today's finest international performing artists, ensembles, and organizations. As a curator and activist for new music and art, she was a founding member of the International Contemporary Ensemble (ICE) and artistic director of MATA Festival (2014–2018), and recently initiated the Pan-Asia Sounding Festival at the National Sawdust. Du Yun was named one of the 38 Great Immigrants by the Carnegie Foundation in 2018. Homepage: www.channelduyun.com

**Pamela Z** is a composer/performer and media artist making works for voice, electronics, samples, gesture-activated MIDI controllers, and video. She has toured throughout the US, Europe, and Japan. Her work has been presented at venues and exhibitions including Bang on a Can (NY), the Japan Interlink Festival, Other Minds (SF), the Venice Biennale, and the Dakar Biennale. She has composed scores for dance, film, and chamber ensembles (including Kronos Quartet and Eighth Blackbird). Her awards include the Rome Prize, Foundation for Contemporary Arts, MIT McDermott Award, the Guggenheim, American Academy of Arts and Letters, and Robert Rauschenberg Foundation. Homepage: www.pamelaz.com

**Jingyi Zhang** is a Ph.D. candidate in musicology at Harvard University. As a music and cultural historian, her research interests center on themes of racial identity, mobility, media technology, and decolonial thinking in 19th to 21st century songs, opera, and theater. Her dissertation, *The Hypermobility Turn: Opera of The Future, The Future of Opera*, was awarded two prizes from the American Musicological Society (AMS), supported by the Holmes/D'Accone Dissertation Fellowship from the AMS, the Virgil Thomson Fellowship from the Society for American Music, the Victor and William Fung Fellowship, and was honored as a finalist for the Harvard Horizons Scholars program. Her publications range from opera and dramaturgy to cultural mobility, decolonial thinking, social activism, Asian diasporic composers, and film music. They appear in the *CHINOPERL: Journal of Chinese Oral & Performing Literature, Sound Stage Screen, The Theatre Times, The Palgrave Handbook of Music in Comedy Cinema,* and is forthcoming in *Jazz and Culture*. Homepage: www.jingyizhangpiano.com

# Acknowledgments

I am honored to work on this edited volume with the invitation and support of Series Editor of Routledge *Focus on Dramaturgy* Magda Romanska. This project was recognized and funded by the Transmedia Arts Seminar from the Mahindra Humanities Center, the Holmes/D'Accone Dissertation Fellowship from the American Musicological Society (AMS), and the Virgil Thomson Fellowship from the Society for American Music (SAM). I would like to express my gratitude to Professors Carolyn Abbate and Kate van Orden of Harvard University, who have been an immense source of inspirational support, and the anonymous peer reviewers who offered invaluable comments on this project. Special thanks are also due to Claire Margerison, Steph Hines, Swati Hindwan, and Imran Mirza from Routledge for shepherding this volume from start to end. Earlier iterations of this project were presented at the "Spaces of Musical Production/Production of Musical Spaces" conference in 2023 organized by the University of Milan, the "Future of Opera" roundtable panel in 2022 co-sponsored by The Mahindra Humanities Center and MetaLAB (at) Harvard, and the "Glocal Networks and Transmedia Flow of Opera and Multimedia Performances in the 21st-Century" roundtable panel at the *21st Quinquennial International Musicological Society Congress* held in Athens.

I am heartened to have the opportunity to collaborate with so many creative artists on this project, who have inspired me as a scholar. This volume would not have been possible without them. Together, this series of chapters is testament to the intriguing and fertile scholarship, which continues to invigorate the study of contemporary opera in the global context.

# Introduction

## Contemporary Opera and New Dramaturgies

*Jingyi Zhang*

*New Dramaturgies of Contemporary Opera: The Practitioners' Perspectives* is the first study that approaches opera dramaturgy from the unique perspectives of living practitioners (composers, librettists, directors, producers, singers, dramaturgs, and administrators) who provide valuable first-hand insight into the genesis of operas in a global context today. As opposed to a typical scholarly book, this project promotes a kind of vernacular thinking intended to capture the ethos of contemporary opera-making in the twenty-first century, which is characterized by a greater commitment to diversity, equity, and inclusion, the integration of new media practices, and more interdisciplinary conversations and collaborations.

These opera practitioners therefore offer an excellent vantage point from which to understand a cornucopia of dramaturgical issues in contemporary operas, ranging from new initiatives to cultivate the next generation of opera creatives, the dramaturgical power of time in an opera, the opportunities and challenges of foregrounding non-Western stories and music, how the environment is presented and re-presented in an operatic performance, and the influence of transmedia and AI technologies on operas today. Opera producers are often faced with many pragmatic and financial challenges, which were aggravated during the global pandemic. In navigating between creative idealism and the realities of a production, they have to be resourceful in order to continue making and producing operas, while at the same time procuring new ideas from the transmedia, gaming, and tech industries to attract new audiences. This fluidity in exchange, improvisatory ethos, and creative spirit that are unfolding in today's operatic ecology have yet to be investigated and reflected upon. This volume thus serves as an intervention in addressing this wide array of heterogeneous dramaturgical practices that go into the making of contemporary operas in an era of flux.

The chapters are organized around four major themes in contemporary opera discourse, beginning more broadly with New Dramaturgical Considerations, which illuminates the behind-the-scenes process necessary for bringing an opera to fruition and offers valuable insights on various on-the-ground challenges faced by opera practitioners in the twenty-first century. This is then

DOI: 10.4324/9781003462286-1

followed by a section on Representing Non-Western Cultures and Perspectives, which not only wrestles with opera's race problem throughout history but, more importantly, raises new questions and suggests new ways of moving beyond the western colonial framework through a critical engagement with a constellation of contemporary operas and radical reimaginations of canonic repertoire. The next section on Site-Specific Dramaturgies addresses the recent emergence of operas staged in alternative spaces, a longstanding practice in the field of theater and performance art but which has recently made its way into opera. No longer existing at the margins of the operatic ecology, site-specific events push for a reconsideration of vocal expression and new media in contemporary opera, as well as lay bare the impossible tensions that are at work. The final section on Creative Possibilities of Transmedia Dramaturgy investigates the prevalent use of new media in global operatic practices today, particularly focusing on the collaboration of multiple platforms, also known as transmedia storytelling in opera.

## New Dramaturgical Considerations

The first section outlines new dramaturgical considerations in contemporary operas today, as we approach it from multiple perspectives: a dramaturg and librettist, a composer, and a producer. These diverse points of view set the stage for our extended investigation of the capacious forms dramaturgy takes in opera, which gestures to its collaborative nature.

Librettist, dramaturg, and translator Kelley Rourke's chapter "Washington National Opera's American Opera Initiative: The First Ten Years" reviews the successes and challenges of the opera company's AOI initiative, which aims to cultivate the next generation of aspiring opera producers. Approaching from the perspective of an AOI mentor herself, Rourke draws on many personal interviews with mentors like Jake Heggie, Mark Campbell, Robert Ainsley, Francesca Zambello, and Teresa Perotta, as well as an online ethnographic survey that documents the experiences of AOI alumni. Rourke illuminates the benefits gained from participating in this key initiative and the critical skills that are necessary today in creating a contemporary opera.

My interview with creative producer of contemporary opera Beth Morrison sheds light on the role of a producer and the dynamism Beth Morrison Projects (BMP) brings to the operatic ecology today. We discuss the pragmatic logistics involved in putting together an opera today, particularly focusing on how Indie Opera companies are navigating this competitive scene, and speculate on whether the new formats that PROTOTYPE 2021 festival pivoted to during the pandemic have effectively prompted a re-envisioning of the artform. Morrison also shares her views on the qualities she looks out for in the new generation of opera creators. Specific operas discussed include Huang Ruo and Basil Twist's *Book of Mountains and Seas* (2021), Ellen Reid's *Prism* (2018), and David Little's *Black Lodge* (2023).

Composer David T. Little's chapter "Seeking the Philosopher's Stone: On the Alchemy of Time in Creative Dramaturgy" takes up the idea of time, and the critical role composers play in accelerating, slowing, or even stopping audiences' experience of time in an opera, not unlike the working of alchemy as he posits. He poses the fundamental question of whether the dramatic arts can indeed alter reality, and from here on, he attempts to answer this question peripatetically by drawing on the writings of Edward Bond, Louis Andriessen, Werner Herzog, Carlo Levi, and Italo Calvino while interweaving examples from his own operas and the music of others. Little offers a provocative contemplation on the magical, irrational power time wields over us. Specific operas discussed include Little's *JFK* (2016), *Soldier Songs* (2006/11), *SIN-EATER* (2023), and *Dog Days* (2012).

## Representing Non-Western Cultures and Perspectives

Having provided an overview of major dramaturgical concerns that are unique to contemporary operas today, the second section examines the representation of non-western cultures and perspectives on stage. The historically marginalized voices of composers are prominent in this section, for they play a critical role in challenging essentialist perceptions of non-Western settings, music, and ideas in their operas.

Composer Kamala Sankaram's chapter "Musicalizing the World: Dramaturgical Considerations of Non-European Culture in Contemporary Opera" approaches musical dramaturgy in the operas of three non-White composers: Anthony Davis, Huang Ruo, and herself. She first traces opera's long history of representing exotic cultures before illuminating the hybrid approach non-White composers undertake in their operas. Drawing on personal interviews conducted with Davis and Huang, Sankaram lays bare stereotypical assumptions held by audiences and commissioners who anticipate familiar exotic tropes. Non-White composers, including herself, who depart from these musical stereotypes are thus often met with a newer form of exoticism. Case studies engaged here include *X: The Life and Times of Malcolm X*, *An American Soldier*, and *Thumbprint*.

My chapter "Interrogating Operatic Decolonization in the Hypermobility Turn: The Industry's *Sweet Land*" illuminates how decolonial thinking is manifested in operas conceived in what I call the *hypermobility turn* to describe a new era of operas that are predicated on breaking barriers, hierarchies, and conventions. I examine the accusatory architecture of *Sweet Land* and its strategies of unsettling before asking new questions about representation and *representability* as reflected in the casting decisions. Then, I turn to *Twilight: Gods* and focus on Scene 4 ("Siegfried's Funeral March") to argue that a new form of musical essentialism is perpetuated in this collaboration. Finally, drawing on the lack of closure in *Sweet Land*, I reflect on the fundamental impossibility of opera—and any artform—in envoicing ethical aporia.

My interview with Pulitzer Prize-winning composer Du Yun centers on her recent opera, *Sweet Land* (2020), which she composed with Raven Chacon and is also featured in my previous chapter. I suggest both chapters be read as a pair for readers to understand this innovative site-specific opera from different perspectives. Du and I discuss the role of place in *Sweet Land* and the paired collaboration concept that shapes the creation of the piece, before focusing on major characters in the opera like Jimmy Gin and Makwa. The transfixing coda of *Sweet Land* (which I discussed at length in my previous chapter) motivates me to ask Du what drove her to this unconventional conclusion. Finally, we address the unique challenges a Chinese-American composer faces and Du's thoughts on the decolonial moment in contemporary opera today.

## Site-Specific Dramaturgies

The third section examines several site-specific "operas" and boundary-blurring performances that ask us to re-consider what singing beyond the human means, how the performance space influences vocal singing and our understanding of it, the multi-faceted ways in which nature gets interwoven into an operatic performance, and how the global lockdown during the pandemic prompted the birth of a site-specific piece resembling a radio opera. The perspectives of a dramaturg, director, and composer/performer are included here because their direct involvement in these unconventional works promotes a re-thinking of artistic concepts and practices we usually take for granted.

Musicologist and dramaturg Jelena Novak's chapter "Landscape Dramaturgy and (Post)opera: Singing After Perspective" draws on dramaturg Ana Vujanović's concept of landscape dramaturgy to shed new light on postopera. Specific examples discussed include the singing ice in a Swedish frozen lake, Hans Werner Henze's *The Raft of the Medusa*, directed by Romeo Castellucci in 2018, and the underwater silent film *Ama* by Julie Gaultier. These idiosyncratic instances of singing beyond the terrestrial—on ice and under water—force a confrontation with postoperatic singing and pose the speculative question of whether voice exists in the absence of breathing. In so doing, Novak aims to arrive at a more expansive understanding of vocal expression in the performing arts today.

Opera and theater director Ashley Tata's chapter "Pastoral Paradox: Staging Ted Hearne's *Farming* (2023) and Kate Soper's *The Hunt* (2023)" examines these two new operas she recently directed that employ nature as both staging and inspiration. Adopting a first-person descriptive account of several moments in the operas, Tata illuminates the opportunities, challenges, and hypocrisies involved in engaging with these sites as performance spaces. Furthermore, Tata draws on the libretti, her extended involvement in the development process, and historical understandings of the pastoral genre in order to shed light on her directorial visions.

My interview with Guggenheim recipient and Rome Prize-winning composer/performer and media artist Pamela Z takes a deep dive into two of her genre-defying "operas," *Times³* and *Wunderkabinet*, the former being a site-specific sonic piece conceived during pandemic times as part of the PROTOTYPE 2021 festival, and the latter co-composed with Matthew Brubeck with video by Christina McPhee. We discuss key motivations and influences driving both works, the challenges involved in making them, and reflect on the character of Alemap Z (Pamela Z in reverse), sung by Pamela Z herself, who sings in reverse in *Wunderkabinet*. In closing, she shares with us her thoughts on how the development of technologies in recent years, accelerated by the pandemic, has fueled the rise in interdisciplinary exchanges between opera and new media.

## Creative Possibilities of Transmedia Dramaturgy

Our final section engages with the creative possibilities of transmedia dramaturgy, a timely subject matter in contemporary operas today, with the increase in collaborations with the tech and gaming industries. This interdisciplinary topic thus necessitates contributions from scholar-practitioners who are directly involved in the creation of these technologically advanced operas and versatile performers who are working at the intersections of the old and the new, not only in terms of repertoire but also in terms of vocal techniques, acting, and new dramaturgies.

Krisztina Rosner's chapter "Transmedia, Tradition, and Music in Contemporary Japanese Performing Arts" engages with the rising phenomenon of transmedia opera, which refers to operas created using multiple platforms. Focusing on the Japanese performing arts scene, Rosner draws on a broad range of case studies to examine the role of transmedia storytelling in operas, including a kabuki rendition of Star Wars called *Star Wars Kabuki – Three Shining Swords*, Shibuya Keiichiro's *The End* performed by the Vocaloid star Hatsune Miku, and two recent Japanese productions of *Madama Butterfly*, which took on vastly different approaches in their radical reimaginations, while making interesting byways to the *INTO* smartphone application and traditional performances like *Chō-kabuki*. In closing, she discusses how an intimate familiarity with local media references is critical to a greater appreciation of transmedia opera in Japan.

Ellen Pearlman's chapter "Biometrics, AI, Embodiment, Performative Practices, and the New Dramaturgy" investigates the recent emergence of AI operas by focusing on three works she participated in: *Noor: A Brainwave Opera (Is There A Place In Human Consciousness Where Surveillance Cannot Go?)*, an interactive immersive brainwave opera, *AIBO: Can an AI Be Fascist? ("Artificial Intelligence Brainwave Opera")*, her second brainwave opera, and *Language Is Leaving Me – A Cinematic AI Opera Of The Skin (Can An AI Have Epigenetic Memories?)*, a cinematic performative installation work. Studying these new artistic innovations alongside historical precedents, most notably the panorama, stereophotography, and Richard Wagner's ideal of the *Gesamtkunstwerk*, Pearlman illuminates how notions like immersion and interaction underlying these practices likewise inform today's innovative artistic practices.

My interview with renowned Israeli contralto Noa Frenkel focuses on her diverse and multifaceted career, as a performer of canonic repertoire and more adventurous contemporary works. Aware of her long-term collaboration with the composer Chaya Czernowin in the operas *Infinite Now* and *Zaïde/Adama*, I ask Frenkel to share with us some of her experiences working with Czernowin, particularly moments of epiphany that impacted her as an artist. We also talk about her role as an actress on stage and the vast spectrum of physicality she has to embrace in channeling various idiosyncratic characters. Other operas discussed include *Prometeo*, *Subnormal Europe*, which is a one-woman opera written for her, and the multimedia work "Solitude in the age of Mass Media." Also known for being an experienced pedagogue of voice, Frenkel discusses her pedagogical vision and approach and concludes our interview with speculations on the future of opera.

This rich constellation of exciting topics in contemporary opera dramaturgy embraces opera as an evolving ecology that lies at the crossroads of the past and the future. Ideally, these four facets of contemporary opera dramaturgy should serve as starting points to motivate scholars and practitioners alike to continue with their own provocative thinking about contemporary opera and performance at large in the twenty-first century and beyond.

# Part I

# New Dramaturgical Considerations

# 1 Washington National Opera's American Opera Initiative

## The First Ten Years

*Kelley Rourke*

### Starting from Scratch: American Opera Initiative Takes Shape

In 2012, Christina Scheppelmann, then Director of Artistic Operations at Washington National Opera (WNO), was troubled by the number of new operas she encountered whose composers had not learned to write for the voice or whose librettists did not know how to structure a story for the operatic stage.[1] Artistic Advisor Francesca Zambello shared her concerns, and the two responded by sketching a two-tier "American Opera Initiative" (AOI): Each year, three early-career teams would receive commissions and mentoring support for 20-minute operas, while a slightly more experienced team would receive a commission for an hour-long opera. All would work with the singers of WNO's Cafritz Young Artist (CYA) program, instrumentalists of WNO orchestra, and members of WNO's staff. Composer Jake Heggie, librettist Mark Campbell, and conductor Anne Manson consulted on program design and served as mentors for early cohorts as they developed their operas from pitch to premiere.

Michael Heaston, whom Zambello brought on to lead the CYA, oversaw AOI as it took shape. Just as AOI composers and librettists learn through real-world experience, Heaston says, AOI's founders learned what worked through trial and error:

> We did not have an explicit formula to begin. I'm proud of us for figuring out a model for something that simply didn't exist. We saw a gap [...] and we just rolled up our sleeves and made it happen.[2]

In order to "make it happen," Heaston and his colleagues needed to identify aspiring opera creators who already had a solid grounding in their own craft, whether musical or literary composition. Originally, the Kennedy Center's Conservatory Project served as the pipeline for composers; drawing on a handful of leading academic institutions not only ensured a baseline of training but also kept the program manageable while it was being created. By 2016, AOI was on a firm footing, and Robert Ainsley, who had succeeded Heaston as leader of CYA/AOI, opened applications to anyone who had not

DOI: 10.4324/9781003462286-3

yet had a major operatic premiere. As word spread, applications increased, and in 2023, 110 composers and 46 librettists applied. Their diverse backgrounds included playwriting, poetry, musical theater, installation art, film, video games, and concert music.

Applications are reviewed by both WNO staff and the mentor team assembled for the cycle in question. Including mentors in the selection process brings in a practitioner's perspective and sets the stage for a productive mentor/mentee relationship. Mentor input also provides an annual "reset" for a review process that is inevitably influenced by individual tastes.

## The Mentor Model: A Dramaturg by Any Other Name

A dramaturg plays an important role in developing a new opera. As Andrew Eggert notes, this role can be filled by "anyone who helps guide development by serving as an advocate for the piece and a catalyst for collaboration, as well as an editor and sounding board for the authors."[3] To fill this role, AOI assigns a composer mentor and librettist mentor each year. These have included composers Anthony Davis, Ricky Ian Gordon, Jake Heggie, Laura Kaminsky, John Musto, Kevin Puts, Kamala Sankaram, and Carlos Simon; and librettists Deborah Brevoort, Mark Campbell, Kimberly Reed, Kelley Rourke, and Gene Scheer. Not only do mentors offer advice on technical details related to their respective specialties but they also provide perspectives on the developing piece as a whole.

The collaborative maelstrom of opera development can be overwhelming, as writers find themselves in dialogue with director, conductor, singers, and staff members. Feedback can be transformative, for better and for worse: For every "a-ha" moment, artists have stories about feedback that distracted them from their original vision or paralyzed them with self-doubt. As Heaston says, "Learning how to filter information and not lose your voice is an important part of the process."[4] Navigating feedback from a producer presents a different power dynamic than navigating feedback in an academic setting. The mentor team is charged with both, offering useful feedback and assisting writers with managing feedback from others.

As a mentor, Heggie leads with questions, prompting the writing teams to imagine the scene on the stage. He says,

> My job is almost like a really good director, imagining the scene on stage. What does the audience know? How do they know it? Why does this happen here? Why this kind of music? Why this feeling? Why this pace? What information is that giving me about the character, about the moment?[5]

By asking these kinds of questions, mentors not only contribute to the development of the work in progress but they also model how composers and librettists can step outside of the concerns specific to their own practice and consider the whole. Heggie describes his approach as "thinking like a director," but he is also modeling what might be described as a dramaturgical skill set. Academic training emphasizes individual practice as young writers gain technical fluency in their disciplines. A program like AOI challenges artists to consider how their work makes space for collaborators to practice their craft.

## The Pitch: What's the Story?

AOI asks composer-librettist teams to begin by collaborating on three "pitches." As writers work through each idea with mentors, two key considerations are the 20-minute time limit and the operatic genre: How will the marriage of words and music serve the story? What makes this story "operatic?" Teams have also been prompted to create operas that speak to the contemporary American experience, but after a few cycles, program staff often saw the teams returning to predictable headline issues again and again.

In 2022, writing teams were not held as strictly to stories of contemporary American life. Jens Ibsen and Cecelia Raker's story of a grandmother who accidentally conjures a demon sprang from their shared interest in the intersection of opera and heavy metal. Silen Wellington and Walken Schweigert wanted to create a mythical shape-shifting character. B.E. Boykin and Jarrod Lee were drawn to a Yoruba tale. Ultimately, since each piece emerged from the sensibilities of artists living in America, they all dealt with "relevant" themes: isolation of the elderly, celebration of the trans experience, and representation of a historically marginalized culture.

Both mentors and alumni consulted for this article recalled conversations about the problems of leading with an *issue* rather than leading with a *story*. One librettist, who is specifically interested in politically engaged work, remembers mentoring around this topic: "Gene Scheer gave us the career-opening advice to go ahead with that (all art is political) as long as we didn't let the tail wag the dog."[6]

As AOI moves forward, identifying and developing operatic stories for today remains a key mentoring area. Story selection and development benefits from mentors' experience and counsel around "what works" in opera, but the most compelling projects begin with a writing team's unique artistic vision and practice. When today's artists are given space for stories they are burning to tell, "relevance" often takes care of itself.

## The Outline: Creating a Shared Space

AOI's founders noted that storytelling for the operatic stage has a specific set of needs. A libretto must contain elements of a strong story, but in such a way that not only allows but also *requires* music for its completion. As the program's founding librettist mentor, Campbell had a clear idea of the method he wanted to teach. "I start with the premise. Then outline, outline, outline, and outline again. If you have a strong outline, the libretto will almost write itself." Because the outline structures not only the libretto but also the opera as a whole, Campbell feels it is important to involve the composer, as well as someone in the producorial role, in the outlining process.

Heggie is also a proponent of front-loading the collaborative process. He describes his long-term collaboration with Gene Scheer as follows:

> We talk endlessly about the story, character journeys, emotional pillars, and touchstones. What inspires each of us. Particular lines or events that excite our imaginations. All of that before anything is written. The scaffolding has to be really clear.[7]

Outlining creates a shared space—a core subject—before the creators become absorbed in technical details of their own work. Educator Parker J. Palmer speaks about "the subject-centered classroom" in which teachers and students gather around a "great thing" with an independent voice. He writes,

> When a great thing speaks for itself, teachers and students are more likely to come into a genuine learning community, a community that does not collapse into the egos of students or teachers but knows itself accountable to the subject at its core.[8]

The subject of discussion is the *opera*—not the libretto, not the music, but the thing that the team will bring into existence together. AOI has further modeled the shared space by involving both mentors at every stage of the process. A librettist mentor may have questions for the composer, while a composer mentor may have advice about language. Finally, the outlining phase is an important time for WNO leadership to weigh in with questions or concerns about the evolving piece before the writing process gets too far along, since once the score is underway, there is little time for major structural revisions.

## Things Get Real: The Workshop

After the outline is complete, AOI's timeline allows about three months each for development of the libretto and first draft of the score, with designated periods for discussion/rewrites appropriate to each phase. In September, writing teams and mentors meet in DC for a four-day piano/vocal workshop with CYAs and WNO music staff. Each piece is allotted a daily 60- to 90-minute session with singers, after which writing teams retreat to work on changes, which are implemented the following day.

"I didn't understand the value of the four-day workshop until I had been through one," said Ainsley. He elaborates,

> I had never done a workshop where we had *talked*. In my past workshop experiences, at Minnesota Opera and Opera Theatre of Saint Louis, we rehearsed the piece, read it down, and recorded it. I had never had time to play, and change, and discuss the *why*s and the *if*s.[9]

Some of the discoveries are technical. For instance, re-barring a phrase may make it easier for singers to find their cue or thinning accompaniment may bring a *pianissimo* line into focus. Questions from singers reveal moments when there is not enough information about stories or characters. Comic timing gets road-tested and refined. One composer remembers learning that the stakes for the main character were not landing; in response, he and his collaborator overhauled the text and music for her final aria.[10]

## Performers as Collaborators

AOI composers write for specific singers from the CYA rather than a theoretical idea of, say, a lyric soprano. In the process, they learn that writing for voice is never as straightforward as writing for clarinet. Zambello describes AOI and CYA as having a symbiotic relationship:

> Composers learn to write for singers by writing for singers, and singers learn to be better artists by working directly with creators. They get to ask questions about why something was written in a certain way. Maybe they'll get an illuminating answer, or maybe the question will make the writers realize they need to make something clearer. I want singers to develop the habits of inquiry and communication. I hope they'll go on to do a lot of new opera, but even if they don't, these are important skills.[11]

Many productive discussions have begun with a question about the quality of sound a composer is seeking, followed by a singer's explanation about what area of his or her range will achieve (or thwart) that effect. Soprano Teresa Perotta, who created roles in both *Bubbie and the Demon* (2023) and *Forever* (2024), says that AOI has not only given her the opportunity to practice collaborating with creatives but also challenged her to expand her own technical tool kit:

> It becomes a conversation among the three of us about the kinds of vocal colors that are possible. I've learned new things I can do with my voice. Not extended techniques, exactly, but approaches to diction and colors. I have more tools now.[12]

A vibrant opera ecosystem requires performers who are equipped to engage with creators. In addition to the musical and dramatic training that has long been standard, the next generation of singers will need to practice engaging in dialogue with creators, and AOI offers one forum to do so.

## Assessing Returns on a Decade of Creative Investment

WNO has invested significant resources in the development of creative talent in the last decade. Besides the shorter works commissioned for AOI, it premiered *The Lion, the Unicorn, and Me* (Jeanine Tesori/J.D. McClatchy), a revised version of *Appomattox* (Philip Glass/Christopher Hampton), and *Grounded* (Jeanine Tesori/George Brant). Of the seven-hour-long operas commissioned under the auspices of AOI, six have been taken up by other companies, including Missy Mazzoli and Royce Vavrek's *Proving Up* (2018), with 16 productions to date, and Kamala Sankaram and Jerre Dye's *Taking Up Serpents* (2019), with four. Of the 20-minute operas, more than a third have been picked up by other companies.

The one-hour opera went on hiatus after 2019 for budgetary reasons but the 20-minute commissions continue. In late 2023, 20-minute opera alumni completed an online survey about their experiences with the program. Telephone interviews with selected mentors and staff provided perspective on AOI's goals and practices as the program moved from a novel idea to an established model.

## A Community of Creators

In their survey responses, alumni highlighted the benefits of being connected with mentors. They also valued connections with collaborators, singers, and WNO staff. Key lessons imparted by mentors included story mechanics (seven responses), character building (five), dynamics of collaboration (five), operatic structure (five), setting text to music (three), opera orchestration (two), writing text that "sings" (two), and writing for the operatic voice (one).[13]

While the AOI commissions are the primary focus of mentorship, more than half of the respondents said mentors provided guidance on general principles they have taken into subsequent work. According to one librettist, "AOI gave me a huge advantage in learning how to support composers' brightest visions and singers' best performances through creating big moments with sparse and intentional text."[14] A composer says,

> I'm now able to ask for more from my librettists (especially in terms of structure), how to make more specific and constructive asks when something isn't working for me, and how to be less defensive when my partner points out something in my work that doesn't work for her.[15]

Approximately half of the respondents (mostly post-pandemic alumni), mentioned that feedback from peers informed their writing process. Until 2021, writers met for the first time at the September workshops. After the pandemic forced the program onto Zoom in 2021, AOI began adding virtual seminars for the full cohort; by the time that cohort met in person, they knew something about one another's work and were better prepared to give each other feedback. AOI's power to create a network (whether mentor/mentee or peer-to-peer) was widely cited as a strength.

A premiere under the auspices of WNO has been another key benefit, both in terms of visibility and skill development. A composer wrote,

> I think the most important aspect was to experience that level of production at an "A-house" company. Learning the expectations and timelines for the production process have been pivotal.[16]

Learning to collaborate efficiently is especially important in a field that brings together large numbers of professionals. Rehearsal time in opera is expensive, and writers receive coaching on how to prepare themselves (and their materials) so they can make the best use of limited time. They also learn what kinds of changes can be achieved at each stage of the process.

## Putting It Together: Creators, Performers, and Audience

Unlike the painter who steps back from the canvas after months of lonely toil, composers and librettists can have only a partial view of what they have made in the studio. My mentor, the designer/dramaturg John Conklin, says you can't really judge a wig until you see it onstage with the orchestra playing. In opera, by the time all forces come together, it is often too late to adjust the piece itself. Some, like *Madama Butterfly*, rise from the ashes of an unsuccessful premiere in revised form. In other cases, early attempts are set aside, their lessons absorbed and integrated into future work. (Verdi's *Falstaff* likely would not have been possible without *Un giorno di regno*.) Over half of the collaborative teams who gained early experience through AOI have continued to work together, and alumni have gone on to contribute more than 55 operas to the repertory, building on what they learned through their AOI experience.

Conceived as a training ground for composers and librettists, AOI has also benefited not only the CYAs but also WNO's entire staff: Annual productions of brand-new work require a different kind of creativity and support than another production of *La bohème*. Finally, and significantly, General Director Timothy O'Leary notes that regular encounters with new work have shifted audience perception and AOI presentations now sell out.

> I have felt the pendulum swing over the past five or six years. Twenty years ago, audiences were pretty sure they were not going to like new work. We're at a different place now. People are genuinely excited. There is a joy that people feel when they witness the spark of creation.[17]

When AOI was launched, it was the only program of its kind in this country. Ten years later, at least three professional opera companies (Seattle Opera, Opera Theatre of Saint Louis, and Atlanta Opera) offer annual micro-commissions. Other companies are getting to know creators by offering readings of existing works in progress. Still others have invested in long-term residencies that culminate in premieres.

## Conclusion

WNO leaders launched AOI as a response to perceived deficiencies in composers and librettists' academic training. As AOI has taken shape, it has become clear that some skills—whether writing music for the voice or stories for the stage—are best practiced not in a conservatory studio but in a professional collaborative environment in which artists learn to collaborate not only with each other but also with all the departments of an opera company. AOI has consciously made space for artists to practice collaborative skills, with strategies that include mentorship, a detailed timeline with designated periods for discussion and revision at every step, a workshop with time for trial and error, and an ongoing dialogue between creative and performing artists. In any commission project, whether composers and librettists are fresh from conservatory or more advanced in their careers, they will likely benefit from this kind of skill-building and support around the multiple collaborative relationships at play in opera creation.

## Notes

1 Christina Scheppelmann, telephone interview with the author, December 1, 2023.
2 Michael Heaston, telephone interview with the author, December 6, 2023.
3 Andrew Eggert, "The role of the dramaturg in the creation of new opera works," in *The Routledge Companion to Dramaturgy*, ed. Magda Romanska (New York: Routledge, 2016), 354.
4 Michael Heaston, telephone interview with the author, December 6, 2023.
5 Jake Heggie, telephone interview with the author, December 5, 2023.
6 Response to author's online survey of AOI alumni, November–December 2023.
7 Jake Heggie, telephone interview with the author, December 5, 2023.
8 Parker J. Palmer, *The Courage to Teach: Exploring the Inner Landscape of a Teacher's Life* (San Francisco: Jossey-Bass, 1997), 120.
9 Robert Ainsley, telephone interview with the author, November 29, 2023.
10 John Glover, interview with the author, January 6, 2024.
11 Francesca Zambello, telephone interview with the author, December 2, 2023.
12 Teresa Perrotta, telephone interview with the author, December 6, 2023.
13 Responses to author's survey of AOI alumni, November–December 2023.
14 Response to author's survey of AOI alumni, November–December 2023.
15 Responses to author's survey of AOI alumni, November–December 2023.
16 Response to author's survey of AOI alumni, November–December 2023.
17 Timothy O'Leary, telephone interview with the author, December 8, 2023.

# 2 Interview with Beth Morrison

*Beth Morrison and Jingyi Zhang*

*JZ:* Being a creative producer of contemporary opera and music theater is such an immense role that's so vested in the process itself, but not always very visible, which makes it mysterious in a way. Can you share with us more about your role, and how it overlaps and differentiates from your company (Beth Morrison Projects [BMP])'s role?

*BM:* Sure, I like the mysteriousness. I think that's a great word. My role and BMP's role are not only related to each other but also separate. When a lead artist—usually the composer—pitches me a project that I'm interested in, we will often have a conversation, focusing on why *this* project, why *now*, and what makes it relevant? And that's always a starting question for me because as a producer of contemporary opera, it must be a work that resonates with contemporary society.

Then, once we've decided to go forward with this idea, I will set the composer up on "dates" with three to five potential librettists to sit with and learn their work, and see if their personality is a fit (unless the composer already knows who to work with). After the librettist is decided, typically the librettist and composer will approach me with ideas on who the director might be, or again, I'll set up artistic "dates" for them to meet and talk to several potential directors in person. The same process applies in the selection of designers. These are very instinctual decisions. It's about knowing who the composer is, what's important to them, how they work, their personality, etc. and finding them the ideal match. We're also really devoted to trying to ensure that we have diversity on our creative teams. And once the director is chosen, we start creating the piece, and the process begins typically with the text. And oftentimes, I'll bring in the music director at the beginning.

We establish a timeline on when to receive the first draft of an outline, particularly if it's a first-time librettist, and we all read through it, before approving it. Then, we get to the first draft and hold our first libretto workshop. We divide up the parts and read

DOI: 10.4324/9781003462286-4

through them. Sometimes the librettists want to read themselves. At times the creative team wants actors to do it. These are the necessary steps I carry out with every project. So, my job is to figure out the process that will lead to the best work by a librettist at this stage. It's not a cookie-cutter approach.

When we get through to a satisfactory final libretto, we go into the music composition phase. And as a creative producer, once again, I have to figure out what would work best for the composer, which typically involves undergoing a series of different (piano/vocal or fully orchestrated) workshops. If the particular composer writes to full score immediately, then having a piano/vocal workshop isn't that helpful. I'll then look for workshopping opportunities with a full chamber orchestra, with about 15 instrumentalists and under. Ellen Reid's *Prism* (2018/2019 Pulitzer Prize for Music) is a great example. She wanted to construct different soundworlds for each act, so she approached the first workshop as an opportunity to try out the various soundworlds. She wrote ten minutes of each act, and Arizona State University School of Music brought their students to it, in a fully orchestrated workshop. It was an incredibly fruitful workshop because she learned this soundworld works for this and not that, and she had to tweak some things here and there, etc. Afterward, we did a full workshop on all the acts spaced out over the years. This is critical for both the composer and creative team to get a chance to hear how things are going. Is the dramaturgy working out both text-wise and music-wise? Is the vocal writing singable for the voice type? How is it all coming together? The series of workshops over a period of three to five years is to ensure that by the time we get to the full rehearsal period before the world premiere, the piece has worked out all the kinks. These workshops are generally attended by composer, librettist, dramaturg, director, and me as creative producer.

The way BMP works is we partner with academic institutions, whether that's a conservatory or university, to do these different workshops. It's a wonderful way of working because part of BMP's mission is to nurture and train the next generation. Working with students enables them to participate in the process of creating a new work, and collaborate with a living composer, which is such a rare opportunity for them. And for us, as members of the creative team, we get to hear the work live and work on the music and texts that we have at that time. So that's typically how BMP works, and my job as creative producer in the development process is really trying to help clarify the overall vision.

With regard to the dramaturgical aspects, oftentimes we work with a director early on, who serves as the dramaturg, and sometimes we'll work with an actual dramaturg. But the creative team is collectively thinking dramaturgically and asking dramaturgical questions starting from the early development stage. Then once we're heading into production, it's a conversation with the creative team about how to realize our vision.

Next, we get into the rehearsal phase that takes three to four weeks and then a week of technical rehearsals, leading to the premiere. During rehearsals, the director, composer, and librettist work directly with the performers; I try to back off a little at that point and just let them do the work. I come into rehearsals several times a week, but mostly I'm trying to give them space. I don't give much feedback unless something's going off the rails, but generally, at that point, I step back. Then once we get into the technical rehearsals, I must be in the theater with them and see what's being built, what's happening, etc. We gather together for a production meeting every evening to figure out how the tech is going, how ideas are being realized, and how we continue making this work. Just like any other member of the creative team at that point, I'm asking many questions and offering feedback on all design elements, trying to clarify the artist's ideas and see if some things are not quite reading. This is one of my main responsibilities as a creative producer.

What BMP does is to serve as the liaison between all parties by setting all the creative and production meetings. Our director of production is the mediating figure between the director, designer, scenic shops, costume shops, etc. as he shepherds the physical production. Then, we're also doing all the marketing, venue (and venue partner) securing, planning for traveling, accommodation, contracting, financial management, and fundraising. It's a huge operation around any project! We constantly wrestle with issues like how to raise the money, who is going to put up the show, and how do we partner with the venues to get the word out, market, sell tickets, and all of those things. Getting a venue in New York is very challenging. Every project involves so much by way of logistics to get to world premiere. After the world premiere, we're creating documentation, like a full video, trailer, audio, look book, etc. My job at that point switches over to sales, as I try selling the project to presenters or other opera companies who might want to do the project. And so, BMP is also a tour producer. Half of our work are world premieres and the other half is touring the work around the world. There are a ton of logistics involved in touring, which is what my company handles.

*JZ:* You've talked about some major challenges in producing an opera today? Could you speak more broadly on how Indie Opera companies navigate between creative idealism and the realities of production in enabling them to thrive in the competitive operatic scene?

*BM:* BMP is the OG Indie Opera company! Indie Opera companies face the perennial issue of ambition versus the reality of the resources that exist. We have a lot more resources than we did when I founded the company. I believe it's all about the artists whom you're working with. In the very beginning, I was working exclusively with very young artists just coming out of school who had hunger, passion, vision, and were super fresh in how they wanted to create that vision. We supported these artists whom I felt shared an affinity with my vision for Indie Opera, which is to actually create in opera something different, unique, and new. And later, Indie Opera became a widespread term, but it didn't exist when I started. That's something I coined and I love that it's used everywhere now.

And I think the way that we got around the issue of ambition versus resources was to work with really young artists who wanted ultimately to build their professional reputations, so they were willing to put in a lot of work, love, and labor. In fact, that's how BMP worked at the beginning. Initially, nobody knew me in New York. I moved to New York when I founded the company, and I made a decision to do four projects a year because if I only did one, it was going to take forever before anybody understood what I was trying to do. I was fundamentally trying to start something new and to transform the field. It was very challenging to raise money, but I did it, and tried to bring in great young artists who could create something very elegant and cool with little resources. That's how BMP did it at the beginning. I don't know how other companies did it, but for us, that's how I went about it.

*JZ:* That's amazing! PROTOTYPE 2021 festival was shifted to digital format due to the pandemic, which gives rise to new presentation formats for operas. How has the pandemic led to a re-envisioning of the art form, both in terms of producing operas and distributing them? Do you think that digital presentations are here to stay after the pandemic?

*BM:* Yeah, that's a great question. I think that the pandemic led to incredible ingenuity within the field and a lot of out-of-the-box thinking, whether it be digital or otherwise. People were finding new ways to work and bringing it to people. I, personally, am extremely interested in the digital realm for opera but not like The Met: Live in HD. I'm very interested in creating opera film for film. For instance, we made a feature film during the pandemic called *Black Lodge* by David T. Little, which was just nominated for a 2024 Grammy for Best Opera Recording. We filmed on location in a warehouse in Maine, and El Mirage which is a desert outside of Los Angeles. It was an incredible experience! I'm very interested in this medium because there's an access that can be created around digital work, which doesn't exist for live work. Many people don't live in cities where operas are frequently being performed, can't afford to go to an opera, and they don't see opera houses as welcoming to all communities, so they don't feel they belong. I think the digital realm offers unprecedented access to the art form, and there are a number of us in the field who are very interested in continuing the work in the digital sphere. I envision more partnerships happening because it can be really expensive! Increasing accessibility and cultivating collaborations are visions I'm deeply committed to and really excited about.

But I do think—having just been to the OPERA America conference, with the ongoing pandemic, and discontinued funding from the government—that we may be taking some steps backward from the progress that I think has been made in the industry because people are very worried about finances right now. So, they're less interested in taking risks and it's a shame. I hope we can get through this moment because we had made tons of progress pre-pandemic.

*JZ:* You've worked with so many visionary artists and composers in the annual PROTOTYPE festival, which really shake things up! These newer operas and music theater works radically push the boundaries of the art form, with Pulitzer prize-winning operas having emerged from the festival. Can you share with us what it's like working with living composers and artists who're in the early stages of their career? You seem to have a sharp instinct in spotting talent—can you tell us what are some qualities you look out for in these newer operas?

*BM:* Yeah, those two Pulitzer prize-winning operas are two pieces that my company BMP commissioned and produced and then we presented them at our PROTOTYPE festival, which we co-founded with HERE. Nothing is more thrilling than seeing how those pieces have been received. What I look for is a composer who has a singular voice. When I heard Missy Mazzoli, you know, she is 100% unique and her compositional voice is 100% true, but you can also hear her lineage.

The other thing I'm looking for is somebody who instinctually writes theatrically, someone with a sense of drama in the music. All of the young generation composers we've worked with who are leaders in the field, like Missy Mazzoli, Paola Prestini, Ellen Reid, Du Yun, David T. Little, Nico Muhly, and Ted Hearne, they have been core artists of BMP since the beginning. We brought them through their first operas and many of them are still working with us. These composers were interesting to work with because they fundamentally thought about their work in a theatrical way. They understood that it was about theatrical pacing and drama in the music itself, as a way to create an opera theater work. For composers who have never made their first opera, it's very daunting to start the process, but it's my great joy to be able to shepherd young composers like Emma O'Halloran, Mary Kouyoumdjian, and our new BMP: Next Gen finalists, Niloufar Nourbakhsh and Elizabeth Gartman to their first operatic work. Working through that process with them is really joyful because they're excited to put their stamp on this kind of work.

*JZ:* Huang Ruo and Basil Twist's *Book of Mountains and Seas* is a very unique multilingual choral-theater work. Some of it is sung in Mandarin and half in an unfamiliar tongue invented by Huang Ruo, which gives an ineffable, primordial quality to the mythic narratives. Could you comment a little about the multilingual conception of this piece? And what kind of listening experience does it cultivate in listeners, both Chinese and Western?

*BM:* It was Huang Ruo's idea to create this partly in a made-up language and partly in ancient Chinese. For most Western audiences who don't know Chinese, they don't know the difference: They're receiving everything as languages they don't understand. Certainly Chinese-speaking audiences will understand the difference. We have chapter titles in English, which provide a basic premise for each chapter. And I think you're right. This made-up language does have this ineffable, timeless quality to it, and I think that's what Huang Ruo's going for. The Chinese supertitles tell the full story, so if you actually read Chinese, you understand everything. And for those who're there for the experience, this is a very meditative piece. You have to give yourself over to this immersive world in order to be transported and not try to understand it, or think, "oh, this is going on too long," or, "what is this writing," etc. You just have to enter the world to enjoy a transporting experience with it.

*JZ:* You've worked closely with Yuval Sharon before he established The Industry. Recently, he became the artistic director of Detroit Opera and brought in his artistic visions cultivated in The Industry into *Twilight: Gods*. Could you speak more about the operatic ecology today, which is characterized by the increasing exchange between Indie Opera and traditional opera companies? Do you think that's something that's going to happen more often?

*BM:* Yes, I think so. Many Indie Opera companies are being created because there isn't a space for those creators and producers to do innovative work at a larger, more established companies that are more conservative. My hope is that over time, the people who're doing really interesting work in Indie Opera will take over and introduce fresh aesthetics to larger companies with more resources. I think when we're at that point, we're probably looking at some pretty serious changes in the industry, which is exciting.

*JZ:* It seems like the boundary between opera, music-theater, opera-theater, site-specific installation pieces, and vocal-theater has become blurrier in these newer operas. What's your thought on this? Do you think there's a value to preserving these labels?

*BM:* Well, when I started BMP, I knew that I didn't want to call what I was doing opera, because that word posed a huge barrier for many. And so, I started searching for the right word, and that's when I started calling everything opera-theater. Many people use that now as well, but that term started with BMP. I felt music hyphen theater is a term that changes people's perspective. It's not a musical like *Cats* but more of a theater piece. The turn to opera-theater eradicates the assumptions audience members have concerning opera.

Lately, I've taken to calling everything we're doing vocal-theater, which is an even more capacious term. I'm trying to shatter expectations, so it's not about *what* it is. If I don't know what it is, I go into the experience more open and ready to receive it for whatever it is. *Aging Magician* is a great example. It's a vocal-theater work. There's spoken text, chorus, and operatic singing—there's everything in that piece. And so, calling it vocal-theater means that it's sung theater through the voice. And that's what we are.

# 3 Seeking the Philosopher's Stone

## On the Alchemy of Time in Creative Dramaturgy

*David T. Little*

There is a passage from British playwright Edward Bond, which for many years has been central to my understanding of drama. It reads:

> What is drama? There are two cups, one white and one blue. The white cup has a handle. The blue cup has none. We break the two cups and trample and scatter the pieces. We carefully reassemble them. No fragment is left over. There is no crack on the cups, not one sign of breakage, each cup is perfect. But the blue cup has the handle and white cup has none. Drama changes reality.[1]

This idea that art, and specifically drama, can alter reality has helped shape my sense of what dramaturgy is, what it can do, and why it is important. This chapter discusses these ideas, somewhat peripatetically, using examples from my own as well as others' music.

### Seeking the Philosopher's Stone

Dramaturgy has a mysterious quality. Even if you happen to find yourself within the subset of people who have encountered the word itself, they often do not really know what it means or understand what exactly a dramaturg does. And though we, as practitioners, somehow instinctively understand how essential this elusive concept is to the artistic success of a new opera or music theater work, it nonetheless can feel rather sorcerous. Perhaps an apt comparison might be to alchemy.

Indeed when writing opera, one attempts to transform a disparate mixture of elements into metaphorical gold: a successful opera. But there is no philosopher's stone here. No simple or formulaic way to unlock the secrets of the form, to devise this gold.

The act of engaging with this operatic alchemy is what I sometimes think of as "creative dramaturgy." In the broadest terms, creative dramaturgy concerns itself with how an opera is made and not with the traditional domains of historicity, recreation, or reframing in subsequent (post-premiere) productions. To

DOI: 10.4324/9781003462286-5

understand it, one must first interrogate how operas work and how they are put together on both small and large scales simultaneously.

For a composer, these include the many standard musical and dramatic building blocks. On the smallest scale, this concerns how melody, harmony, rhythm, texture, noise, orchestration, and prosody are combined in the score. But larger-scale questions are also engaged with regard to how a piece moves (form, pacing, harmonic rhythm, etc.), how it says what it is trying to say (story framing and narrative approach), and whether through the alchemical commingling of music, text, and form the audience is made to care about the characters on stage. Most vitally—and on the grandest scale—creative dramaturgy involves how we treat or control the audience's perception of the passing of time, i.e., how long or short a piece feels.

An opera composer must consider all of these, at every moment. And to be sure, in failing to consider any single element sufficiently, the composer can make or break an opera. Though Joseph Kerman's notion that "the dramatist is the composer" is out of touch with the current movement to give more and deserved recognition to librettists, there is no denying that it is still the composer who must manage the passing of time in an opera.[2] An insuperably flawed libretto notwithstanding, if an opera feels long or moves too slowly, it is almost certainly a dramaturgical failing of the composer. Composition, in the end, is dramaturgy.

A vital element of this compositional dramaturgy is the metabolism that results from the connubial relationship between music and the story being told. I have always felt that in great opera, the audience is hyperaware of and invested in the music, while simultaneously being so rapt with the drama, storytelling, and characters that they may no longer consciously hear it. One could say that the experience of opera bypasses rational thinking and engages more directly with the subconscious in a powerful way, enabling the audience's awareness of the passing of time to slow or even stop. It offers, as director Werner Herzog suggests, "a direct path to the sublime,"[3] and as anyone who has experienced this can attest, it can be an unforgettable, almost otherworldly experience.

## Stealing Time

The late Dutch composer Louis Andriessen was, for me, among our greatest musical philosophers. His oeuvre explores big ideas like time, matter, death, metaphysics, and politics, and in so doing engages with big thinkers like Plato, Dante, St. Augustine, Aeschylus, Bakunin, Anaïs Nin, Marie Curie, Sor Juana Inés de la Cruz, Lao Tzu, and others. Though perhaps best known for his early politically charged works like *Workers Union*, *De Volharding*, and *De Staat*, Andriessen's work also explored more philosophical and existential themes. (When one attests, as Andriessen did in *De Staat*, that music is powerless to affect social change, how is a politically engaged composer to make sense of the world but to dig deeper into its philosophy?) This inevitably leads to a contemplation of time, intermingled as it is with so many other philosophical concerns.

Time, as the title suggests, is central to *The Art of Stealing Time*, a collection of Andriessen's writings and conversations edited by Mirjam Zegers. In Zegers' introduction, she lays out the prominence of Andriessen's interest in the subject: "With *Contra Tempus*, he looks to the past, in *Anachronie*, he stacks past, present, and future on top of one another."[4] *De Tijd* [Time], draws on text from St. Augustine's *Confessions* to explore "a moment of eternity in sound."[5] In *De Snelheid* [Velocity], "slowness overcomes speed,"[6] suggesting that time is unreliable: pulsing woodblocks shift suddenly to faster tempi, accelerating in each section until they reach their fastest point, then stop: time is momentarily ungoverned. Then the blocks return, resuming their opening tempo, circular, as if nothing had happened: time is unconquerable. *Facing Death*, described by Zegers as bringing "a metaphysical haste to the music,"[7] interprets the famed fast tempi of Charlie Parker's music as a sign of Parker's knowledge of his own mortality. Time and death, like the hourglass and skull of the *memento mori*, feel perpetually linked.

I was fortunate to know Louis toward the end of his life and to feel a sense of mentorship from him. Consequently, the fixation on time in his work proved contagious and I now share his preoccupation, though my conclusions have evolved somewhat differently. At the broadest level, my memory of *The Art of Stealing Time* drifted over the years, reshaping its thesis into "composition is the art of stealing time," which, though inaccurate as a quotation, attracts me very much as an idea. In fact, this incorrect understanding has enabled me to think more deeply about time in the context of opera and music theater, and how this relates to the audience.

"Just as the painter appropriates colour, so the composer steals time at will," Zegers notes. "In exchange for the theft, time takes a work, stolen time becomes fixed time […] The passing of time is the only thing which all music has in common. Timeless music does not exist."[8] And yet we often refer to music as "timeless." For me, Gustav Mahler's *Urlicht*—in the hands of the right conductor—possesses this quality. It is something to which I also aspire in my own work and consider this quality to be an essential element in any successful operatic composition.

For Louis, Mahler rather objectionably did not "keep to the limitations imposed on him by musical time," but instead stole "*real* time."[9] For me, the ability of music to steal *real* time is a curious virtue, particularly in the manner here attributed to Mahler. Indeed, if music can *shape* our perception of time (which ironically both Mahler and Andriessen have proven), then perhaps it can also, in some metaphorical way, *stop* time. And if we can stop time, perhaps we can also cheat death. (Again, the skull and hourglass.)

## Cheating Death

The Italian painter and writer Carlo Levi said,

> Death is hidden in clocks…every means and every weapon is valid to save oneself from death and time. If a straight line is the shortest distance between two fated and inevitable points, digressions will lengthen it; and if these digressions become so complex, so tangled and tortuous, so rapid as to hide their own tracks, who knows—perhaps death may not find us, perhaps time will lose its way, and perhaps we ourselves can remain concealed in our shifting hiding places.[10]

Levi is discussing Lawrence Sterne's digression-rich *Tristram Shandy,* and like many, I first encountered the passage in Italo Calvino's *Six Memos for the Next Millennium*. In this insightful collection of lectures, Calvino discusses concepts he felt were vital to literature and which also apply to drama: lightness, quickness, exactitude, visibility, multiplicity, and consistency. It is in the discussion of quickness that these lines of Levi are quoted and Calvino retorts:

> Because I am not devoted to aimless wandering, I'd rather say that I prefer to entrust myself to the straight line, in the hope that the line will continue into infinity, making me unreachable […] that I will be able to launch myself like an arrow and disappear over the horizon…[11]

These quotations might at first glance appear to be in opposition, presenting two divergent approaches to storytelling and dramaturgy: one straight and one meandering. Yet both speak to art's power to alter our perception of time and ultimately cheat death by making ourselves unreachable by it. In this, they coexist, if in counterpoint. Calvino himself supports this reading with a personal meditation on the Latin phrase *Festina lente* or "hurry slowly" in particular, as represented by the publisher's mark of Aldus Manutius showing a dolphin curved around an anchor: "I have always preferred emblems that throw together incongruous and enigmatic figures," he notes, as "between them [they] establish an unexpected kind of harmony." Levi's meandering (which I also consider as a circle) and Calvino's straight line share a similarly unexpected kind of harmony.

Aspects of these ideas can be found in nearly all of my operas, but they are perhaps most explicit in my grand opera *JFK* (2016),[12] a work that delves into the final 12 hours of President John F. Kennedy's life, before his assassination in Dallas. A work quite explicitly about the desire to cheat death, *JFK*, more than any other of my works, attempts to hide from death in its layers, "concealed in our shifting hiding places" as Levi puts it.[13] In this, Acts I and II are full of detours: morphine-induced dream states shared by John F. and Jackie Kennedy bring us first to the surface of the moon, with moments both serene and surreal; then to haunting specters from the time of Lincoln; and finally to an encounter between Jackie and her future self.

It's a phantasmagorical work that relishes in a sense of timeless beauty, allowing us to believe that we, in fact, can hide from death, even as characters representing the Three Fates remind us that we cannot. Though not overlong—the first half lasts only 77 minutes—it nonetheless takes its time through these detours and, in the spirit of the grand opera, ruminates in arias, duets, and trios.

But then something changes. In the third act, following what is perhaps its most expansive and time-stopping moment—a grand *Rosenkavalier* trio setting to music Alan Seeger's poem "I Have a Rendezvous with Death"—things begin to accelerate in a curious manner. Scenes grow shorter and the work overall seems to push forward, even as the music itself grows mostly slower. A series of brief scenes shows the Kennedy's concluding business, stealing brief affectionate moments together, and being readied for departure, while the music seems to try to hold us back. This is especially true in the final two arias, "If You Knew" and "A Lucky Man." I wanted it to feel as if the opera itself is trying to resist the inevitable.

While composing *JFK*, I became fascinated by a concept from Lars von Trier's *Melancholia*: that as the eponymous rogue planet approached its collision with Earth, it appeared to alter the latter's sense of gravity. I wanted the audience to feel a similar sense of cosmic alteration as they approached Kennedy's assassination: to feel the drastic inevitability of his fate (and ours) even as the detours of the first half had falsely suggested that we could delay it.

"Death is hidden in clocks," Levi tells us, and that "a straight line is the shortest distance between two fated and inevitable points."[14] *JFK*'s third act uncoils its initial digressions and straightens into this line. Here, the clock reigns. It is no accident that the accompaniment for Jack's final aria, "A Lucky Man," consists of pointillistically-orchestrated piano, vibraphone, and harp, ticking away quarter notes at ♩= 60. Here, dramatic time and real time merge, as both Kennedy's and the audience's seconds align and tick down. Dramaturgically, the audience should be unaware of this merger; perhaps- they sense it but are unable to consciously identify it. Like death, the awareness of fate should come like a thief in the night.

It was always my conceit that the assassination of John F. Kennedy holds an uncomfortable mirror to our own mortality. Here, as dramatic time and real time merge, this point is driven home, as Jack sings, "I'm a lucky man, time has been kind to me. Well, mostly kind." Periodically in this section, the strings will end a phrase with a short downward glissando, almost like a sigh, suggesting perhaps an attempt to break free from time toward an approaching eternity. Each time, however, the ticking quarter note grid reasserts itself and forces the strings back in place.

Following his aria, Jack exits but the chorus remains. Staring out at the audience, they interrogate the nature of a person's last words. The violins (now *divisi a 17*) then finally break free. Though still linked to the ticking clock in their entrances, their sinking glissandi start to extend for several bars, blurring time as if it were melting toward eternity. It is amidst this passage that the Fates begin their final phrase with the pointed lyric, "he's gone." The audience left with no place to hide—no more detours, only fate. It is a moment that has always brought to mind for me the passage from Michel de Montaigne, which also serves as an inscription in the score's front matter:

> But in that last scene played between death and ourself there is no more feigning; we must speak straightforward French; we must show whatever is good and clean in the bottom of the pot...[15]

## Returning Time

I take a different approach to time in some of my other operas: *Soldier Songs* (2006/2011), an opera in the form of a song cycle that explores the cost of war on those who fight it; *Black Lodge* (2019),[16] ritual opera-theater, which asks how far into darkness one can go before a return is no longer possible; *SIN-EATER* (2023), a ritual grotesquerie for choir and string quartet that interrogates the relationship between food and power. Reexamining the operatic form itself, these works explore complex subjects through a kind of triangulation of snapshots: abstract characters ("the soldier," "the inheritor," or simply unnamed characters[17]) perform relatively short scenes expressing specific and varying viewpoints (rather than longer, traditional dramatic scenes), which accumulate (in part through their juxtaposition) to create what we'd traditionally refer to as the work's narrative.[18]

I view this as a distillation of the operatic form. Herzog writes that "feelings [in opera] are so abstracted; they cannot really be subordinated to everyday human nature any longer, because they have been concentrated and elevated to the most extreme degree and appear in their purest form."[19] Through this distillation and the resulting compression of dramatic logic, I likewise try to further concentrate and elevate operatic feelings, pursuing Herzog's "path to the sublime" in the most direct way possible.

In this, my primary concern is with emotional impact, and I accept that the "story" itself may remain less clear, the specifics subject to debate. For works written in the 21st century and which are primarily interested in raising questions rather than giving answers, this feels not only acceptable but also appropriate. It is my hope that the emotional impact of these works will encourage the audience to contemplate the topics raised by the sometimes-ambiguous plot long after the performance has ended.

Integral here is a deep interest in how this formal approach impacts our sense of the passing of time and allows real time to feel shorter than dramatic time. These works typically seem longer in the memory than the number of minutes they actually lasted. Rather than stealing time, these works might be considered to return time to the audience.

This approach has its roots for me in youthful encounters with works like Faulkner's *As I Lay Dying* and John Zorn's *Naked City*, both of which engage with memory, fragmentation, and form in innovative ways. And likewise with the cut-up techniques of Brion Gysin and William S. Burroughs, an aleatory technique in which text is cut into fragments and then rearranged to create a new text. Burroughs felt that the prose resulting from the cut-up processes could often speak of events that had not yet occurred, thus predicting the future, declaring in 1976, "when you cut into the present, the future leaks out."[20] This mystical notion would become very important to me in the creation of *Black Lodge*.[21]

Luciano Berio's music is also important here: works like *Recital I (for Cathy)* or "*Points on the curve to find...*". (The evocative title of this latter work often feels like a way to describe my distilled narrative approach.) And of course his *Sinfonia*, the third movement in particular, with its musical representation of non-linear history set against Mahler's linear movement, resonating with me as the coming together of Levi's circle and Calvino's line.

*Soldier Songs*, *Black Lodge*, and *SIN-EATER* are likewise both circular and linear. Musically propulsive, they explore their subjects in a cumulative way, finding one "point on the curve" at a time. Both *Black Lodge* and *Soldier Songs* also end where they began, making their form literally circular and conveying a sense of inescapability. And like in *Naked City*, where short stylistic bursts accumulate in the memory to suggest a sum greater than its parts, these works compress narrative through frequent, sometimes jarring, changes. All roughly an hour in length, the memory of these operas feels more momentous than the duration might suggest, thus they return time. They hurry slowly, meander in a straight line and race in circles around their themes.

## Catharsis, Mystery, Alchemy, and Faith

Sometimes in my work, I pursue a sense of catharsis through the cessation of perceptible musical time. For example, in *Dog Days* (2012),[22] an opera that tells the story of an American family struggling to survive in the face of a catastrophic breakdown of society, leading them to ask where the line between animal and human really lies. In the epilogue of this opera as shown in Figure 3.1 below, after nearly two hours of driving rhythmic music—including several instances evoking clocks—all pulse disappears. A drone from the electric guitar increases in volume and intensity for 12 minutes, a straight line slanting upward, as the other members of the nine-piece orchestra add color and cast off musical sparks. Through sound design, this movement's final minutes become sonically overwhelming, shaking both the theater and the bodies of the audience members within it. Then, in this moment of excruciating timelessness, dramatic time and real time merge, and the clock asserts itself: strings play unison quarter notes at ♩ = 60. They slowly glissando upward, eventually dominating texture: death and time pulse in unholy alliance.

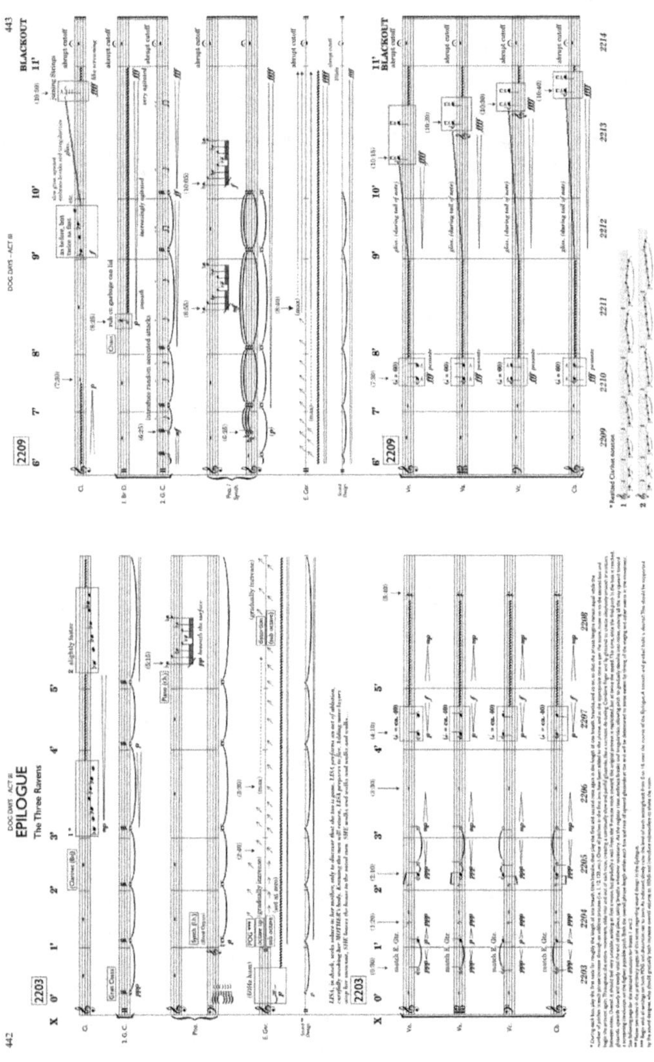


*Figure 3.1 Dog Days* epilogue.

The sensation when this sound cuts off is simultaneously one of exhilaration, terror, and relief, as the cruel truth of the cannibalistic denouement is laid bare just before the blackout.

Likewise in the final movements of *Soldier Songs*, a dissonant progression slowly resolves over ten minutes of drones and groaning reverberant glissandi; gradually the bass drums enter, at ♪ = 60, marking the passing of real and dramatic time with increasing insistence. Unlike in *Dog Days*, this pulse fades, and the oppressive texture melts into something if not hopeful, at least comforting. A sampled soprano sings, "I wish I could tell you that everything will be alright," before a faster coda rushes us toward the end, then back again to the beginning.

Although the final movement of *Black Lodge* is slower than ♩ = 60, there is nonetheless a drone-like quality to the conclusion. Here, several melodies from earlier in the piece are layered contrapuntally, creating a texture that simultaneously relishes a kind of bliss, and yearns for escape. It is perhaps telling that this passage's lyrics begin with "Slow down the clock, unravel the coil that keeps you tight."

In both *Soldier Songs* and *Black Lodge*, a full catharsis is cut short, however. Since each piece is a circle, the audience is unceremoniously returned to the beginning and the piece starts again. Like happy Sisyphus, we approach our boulder, having experienced something cathartic and hopefully having glimpsed something bigger or deeper than ourselves.

Indeed, I have recently come to understand these glimpses as relating to something bigger than dramaturgy: something spiritual that I seem to have been subconsciously pursuing in my work. I am still trying to understand what exactly that means, but it seems to be no accident that my only sacred work, *dress in magic amulets, dark, from My feet*, shares the drone-like quality with the conclusions of *Dog Days*, *Soldier Songs*, and *Black Lodge* (which itself includes a quotation of *magic amulets*). These impulses come from somewhere: just as alchemists sought the philosopher's stone, I am searching for something in creative dramaturgy.

And perhaps alchemy is the perfect conceptual model for this. One of alchemy's goals—besides turning lead into gold—was to produce the "elixir of life." Derived from the philosopher's stone, this elixir would cure ailments and extend life indefinitely. If music can create the feeling of stopped or slowed time, suggesting a metaphorical cheating of death, or create a state of transcendence through catharsis, do we *already* possess a kind of philosopher's stone? An alchemical framework, however loose, may help us understand not only the magical things we feel great opera gives us but also how the mystery of creative dramaturgy can come to feel mystical.

Of course, we are not transmuting lead into gold. Our conscious minds know that music cannot stop time and opera cannot cheat death. These are material matters, not affected by aesthetic ones. Still, I believe Edward Bond that "drama changes reality," even if we understand this only to mean the reality of the mind. (Is there another kind?) And if we at least feel that music stops time, can that be enough? Could we not choose to believe that in that stopped time or cathartic transcendence, we've cheated death, if only briefly? It comes down to faith, I suppose. I know in this case what I will choose to believe.

## Notes

1 Edward Bond, *Plays: 8* (London: Methuen Drama, 2006), x.
2 See Joseph Kerman, *Opera as Drama* (Berkeley: University of California Press, 1988).
3 Werner Herzog and Moira Weigel, "On the Absolute, the Sublime, and Ecstatic Truth," *Arion: A Journal of the Humanities and the Classics* 17, no. 3 (2010): 1–12.
4 Louis Andriessen and Miriam Zegers, *The Art of Stealing Time*, trans. Clare Yates (London: ARC Publications, 2002), 8.
5 Ibid., 8.
6 Ibid., 8.
7 Ibid., 8.
8 Ibid., 11.
9 Ibid., 13.
10 Italo Calvino, *Six Memos for the Next Millennium* (Cambridge: Harvard University Press, 1988), 47. Quoted from Laurence Sterne, *La Vita e Le Opinioni Di Tristram Shandy, Gentiluomo*, trans. Antonio Meo (Turin: Einaudi, 1986).
11 Ibid., 47–48.
12 Subtitled, "an opera in 31 moments with prologue." Libretto by Royce Vavrek.
13 Calvino, 47.
14 Ibid., 47.
15 Michel de Montaigne, "That We Should Not Be Deemed Happy Until After Our Death," in *The Complete Essays*, trans. M.A. Screech, Penguin Classics (London: Penguin, 2003), 85–88.
16 Libretto by Anne Waldman.
17 Contextual choices ensure that the audience will still care about and relate to these characters.
18 While my operas *What Belongs to You* (2021; after the novel by Garth Greenwell) and *Vinkensport*, or *The Finch Opera* (2010/2018; libretto by Royce Vavrek), share characteristics related to this narrative approach, they manifest more with regard to character than to time. I've therefore omitted discussion of these works here, though a longer article could certainly illuminate commonalities across all of my operas.
19 Herzog, 8.
20 William S. Burroughs, *Origin and Theory of the Tape Cut-Ups*; Vinyl, L.P., Album, *Break Through in Grey Room* (Belgium: Sub Rosa, 1986).
21 I am reminded of another William S. Burroughs quotation, which I encountered as a teenager and which no doubt influenced my thinking here. When discussing sudden narrative shifts in *Naked Lunch*, Burroughs is reported to have said, "I'm not American Express. If the reader's asked to take it from Tangiers to Paris in one jump, he'll have to get there himself." See *The Source: The Story of the Beats and the Beat Generation*, DVD (Kino Lorber, 1999).
22 Libretto by Royce Vavrek after the story by Judy Budnitz.

# Part II

# Representing Non-Western Cultures and Perspectives

# 4 Musicalizing the World

## Dramaturgical Considerations of Non-European Culture in Contemporary Opera

*Kamala Sankaram*

### Exoticism and Synthesis

Opera has a long history of depicting "exotic" cultures including India, Africa, Latin America, and even the United States (considered exotic by 19th-century Italian audiences). As Edward Said first suggested, these historical depictions were *not* motivated by attempts to represent the Others accurately. Rather, they represented the perspective of the (usually European) composer looking at the Other. This White gaze, informed by the lens of the majoritarian culture at large, upheld various power dynamics and stereotypical assumptions embedded in that relationship. Said also introduced the notion that this dynamic was cyclical in nature: composers who uncritically draw on tropes found in older works would in turn produce new works that resort to musical essentialism. This, in turn, would lead to the creation of new musical essentialisms as each exoticist work fed into the next.

Ralph Locke (2007) builds on this premise in his writing on exoticism. He suggests that we must also consider the extra-musical contexts that contribute to the sense of exoticism, particularly in narrative forms:

> The words and visual elements in an opera, oratorio, or film place the character or group in a given Elsewhere. Often, the music marks the character or group indelibly as "barbarous," "seductive," "wise," or whatever. The audience melds the two discrete messages into a dissoluble whole [...] Music in these dramatic genres thus helps "characterize"[...] just as it often does when the representation involves madness, supernatural creatures, women, or other conditions, groups, or individuals that have long been viewed as Other, i.e. as departing in some basic way from the heroic, masculine norm.[1]

It is the combination of musical motives with the specific words and actions of the characters in the opera, which gives these stereotypical representations their power. As Locke explains, a depiction of a non-European character may still be exoticized even if it does not quote actual music from the place

DOI: 10.4324/9781003462286-7

being depicted. Rather, the goal of the characterization is to create the sense that this person or place is different from the home country. Ultimately, the larger dramaturgical objective is that the music is *perceived as different* by the people making and receiving the exoticist cultural product.

The contrast, then, between a creator who does not come from a non-European culture and one who does is a difference in assumed frame of reference. If your point of reference is that music from non-European cultures constitutes an unfamiliar Other, it is more likely that you use this music to signify the Otherness of a character. As composers from non-European cultures do not associate the music of their culture with difference and Otherness, they will create their musical characterizations using a less stereotypical set of musical tools.

Furthermore, the methods adopted by contemporary non-White composers are often informed by a dual awareness of the norms of European classical music existing alongside the conventional practices of the non-European culture the composer comes from. This dual awareness will be manifested in a hybrid approach to composition, where the composer attempts to reference his or her cultural background while remaining true to the norms of the European classical style, including the use of classical voices, European orchestral instruments, tuning systems, and linear narrative structures.

Thus, as composers of non-European descent working in the field of opera, our position often begins from a place of musical hybridity. Even for those of us who were raised with an appreciation of European classical music, we are hyperaware of the non-European elements of our backgrounds, which form a parallel foundation in our compositional toolkit. Approaching dramaturgy from a place of hybridity removes the sense of distance from the compositional perspective. Put another way, giving European and non-European compositional techniques equal musical and dramatic weight enables the creation of an integrated whole rather than a composite of hierarchical structures. The mixing of compositional approaches thus serves as an essential part of the musical language rather than as mere signifier for an exotic character or place. Yayoi Everett categorizes this strategy as musical synthesis, where a work "effectively transform[s] the cultural idioms and resources into a hybrid entity."[2] While she is specifically defining this approach in reference to East Asian music, it is applicable to other non-European music as well.

While there is heightened awareness of musical exoticism in opera than there was in the 19th century, it has not gone away. In fact, new genres of exoticism have evolved today, which co-exist alongside older ones. More specifically, this new exoticism is materialized into a set of expectations concerning musical techniques that *should* be employed by non-White composers. While hybridity and syncretism are found in much of the work by contemporary non-White composers, there are also composers who are not interested in employing these techniques at all but feel pressured to reference the "authentic" music of their culture in order to be commissioned and eventually be accepted by the broader public. Thus, new exoticism still represents the ideas of the majoritarian culture as manifested in the often unspoken expectations of what a non-White composer *should* sound like. We can hear direct reflections on both syncretism and the new exoticism from composers Anthony Davis and Huang Ruo.

## Case Study One: Anthony Davis

A recent conversation with composer Anthony Davis illuminates how his approach to writing the music for his acclaimed opera *X: The Life and Times of Malcolm X* (1986) is shaped by the use of jazz as a signifier for Malcom's evolution in thought and to elucidate the variety of rhetorical styles among his other main characters. As Davis describes,

> I never called *X* a jazz opera. I think it certainly uses and [is] inspired by the tradition…because part of the construction of *X* was also thinking about the parallel development of jazz from the late 1940s to the 60s [as it] parallels Malcolm's development as a politician and as leader of a movement… And what was very funny is that when I was analyzing it, I was thinking of Martin Luther King's rhetorical style as opposed to Malcolm's and I always thought Martin was like Coltrane. It was incredibly melodic, charismatic, you know, the Baptist preacher. And when you hear "Alabama," for example, they say that he actually set his Birmingham speech to music. But Malcolm—his rhetorical style was so different, so witty and, and full of surprising turns. And, more mercurial – you know, a different style. And I said, well, he's Miles. That's the Miles pop: the staccato the thing, the rhythmic thing, the sparkle thing. So, when he was doing his speeches, [I] drew upon Miles Davis [as] a big influence. Miles. And it's sort of funny because it was Miles' later [work] like *Brew*.[3]

While the musical motives throughout the opera are constructed using the formal language of jazz, Davis draws on his deep familiarity with the history of the genre to build rich musical depictions of each character by incorporating specific references, ranging from Duke Ellington to McCoy Tyner. Martin Luther King's lyricism is represented in the style of John Coltrane while Malcolm X's sharper oratory draws on the spikiness of Miles Davis's late style. This approach stands in stark contrast to many operas featuring Black characters, whereby the blanket style of "jazz" serves as a signifier for their Blackness and therefore their Otherness. *Porgy and Bess* is one familiar example. Here, even a sympathetic composer like George Gershwin embeds the majoritarian cultural perspective into his musical dramaturgy. He uses jazz harmonies and compositions based on Gullah spirituals to characterize the entire population of Catfish Row. These musical gestures, when paired with the stereotypical actions and behaviors of the characters, end up reinforcing and perpetuating their "Otherness" rather than differentiating them as individual people.

In addition to his background in jazz, Davis developed an interest in Indian classical music and gamelan while he was studying at Wesleyan University. He incorporates elements of Indian tala into the structure of *X* as a device for creating rhythmic cadences that correspond to the overall dramatic structure. These rhythmic gestures are not used to signify India in any way, as he reveals in our interview:

*ANTHONY DAVIS:* So a lot of the formal structure in *X*, from the beginning of the opera, was thought of in these large-scale rhythmic structures… I would have something in 15 [beats] and something in 27 [beats] and where these things would come together it was dramatic. For example, in Act I where the social worker comes in, it's all measured out by how the time structures work.

*KAMALA SANKARAM:* So, the cycle coming together, it's like reaching *sam*[4] in a way?

*ANTHONY DAVIS:* Yeah, exactly. And I try to think about it as these gigantic downbeats: that, where there's a conjunction [between the rhythmic cadences], it's like nodes of a wave. And these were not only musical structural devices, but also dramatic devices.[5]

While Davis does not describe *X* as a "jazz opera," he does acknowledge the fact that the presence of jazz in the opera fulfilled an expectation for the audience in a way that some of his other operas do not. He describes his experience with the science-fiction opera *Under the Double Moon* (1989) in our interview:

*ANTHONY DAVIS:* …the music had these intense rhythmic structures all the way through the opera. Unlike *X*, it wasn't as eclectic. It was very much one part of my music, not trying to say or do a particular thing. Which made it completely different from *X* and I don't think people were ready for it, but that's the way it was.

*KAMALA SANKARAM:* What do you think about that? That you do X and then you do this other thing that's completely different and people aren't ready for it. Do you think there's a certain expectation about what your music is supposed to sound like?

*ANTHONY DAVIS:* Yeah. What the subject matter is supposed to be, too. And what the music's supposed to sound like. I think sometimes they were waiting for the jazz to happen.[6]

## Case Study Two: Huang Ruo

I also spoke with Huang Ruo, composer of *An American Soldier* (2018) and *M Butterfly* (2022), among other operas. Like Davis, Huang's approach to creating Chinese characters does not rely on the use of Chinese scales or melodies as a signifier of Otherness:

*HUANG RUO:* I think it's more character driven. So, even with *An American Soldier*, the mother of Danny Chen was born in Asia and immigrated to [the] US versus Danny, who is 100% American. Because of their difference in background and character, I would write them differently but that's not necessarily [because] this is reserved for Asian characters […] In the end it is still a very personal creation process, that all the characters will bear a voice or a language of the opera universe, which is [what] that opera requires. So what I'm trying to say is that instead of demonstrating contrasts between these characters, they all speak in a very consistent vocal style. Because of the story, drama, and character, there is bound to be subtleties of differences.[7]

One of the striking things Huang Ruo mentioned was the added expectation that, as a Chinese composer, his works should deal with explicitly Chinese subjects:

*HUANG RUO:* I think that it's more abstract with symphonic work. I could create a piece [and] just name it *Symphony Number One*, which is suicidal by the way. I did have a *Symphony Number One*, of course. It was never done anywhere. If they wanted to do a *Symphony Number One*, they would not think of me. But if I have a piece called *Moonlight Meditation* or something very Eastern, suddenly they might be interested to place it in a certain program. So, I think as Asian composers and as minority composers, we are programmed more accordingly with the [theme] of that concert.[8]

Again, an exoticist expectation of what a Chinese composer should be writing directly impacts whether they get commissioned and have their operas performed. Despite this recognition, many non-White composers are indeed drawn to telling stories of their own cultures. The challenge for commissioners and audiences is to allow these composers to tell their stories in the manner they see fit, allowing opera to move past its self-referential reliance on the exoticist tropes of older works. For Huang Ruo, this historical exoticism is part of his motivation for creating operas with Asian subjects.

*HUANG RUO:* So in this case, I willingly put myself in a spot in which I embrace my culture, [the] ability to tell stories of my community, and my cultural background [...] for several reasons. Number one is [that] I remember seeing Asian subjects created but not by Asian composers. Or librettists for that matter. And it was just a White team creating [an] exotic story. [...] So, I just felt how far we have [to move] on from Puccini, or from Gershwin for that matter.[9]

## Case Study Three: Kamala Sankaram

For my last case study, I focus on my own experience creating *Thumbprint* (2014), my first full-length opera, which incorporates a South Asian subject and draws on South Asian musical techniques. *Thumbprint* revolves around Mukhtar Mai, the first woman in Pakistan to win a court case involving an honor crime. She is the founder of the Mukhtar Mai Women's Organization, which works to promote women's rights through education.

As a biracial woman, much of my approach to writing the music for *Thumbprint* reflects an attempt at bridging both sides of my musical upbringing: to combine my training as a composer in the European classical tradition and a classically trained singer with my training in South Asian classical music (specifically, Hindustani sitar) and my childhood spent listening to Carnatic music and Bollywood.

For *Thumbprint*, I was most interested in experimenting with the structural aspects of each musical culture and how those might be synthesized. The melodic and harmonic language of the opera incorporates the Hindustani system of raga. However, my goal was not to try and write a pure piece of Hindustani music. Rather, I utilized the ragas as pitch sets and tone rows from which to build melodic and harmonic progression through the piece. The ragas themselves were chosen for their *rasa*[10] according to how it might support the dramatic arc of each scene. For example, the scenes in which Mukhtar realizes her desire for education are composed around the raga Saraswati, which is for the goddess of wisdom. I was not attempting to create a facsimile of Hindustani music, but produce something that represented both sides of my cultural heritage.

Since *Thumbprint* focuses on a woman finding her voice, the major musical metaphor I utilized was developed through my vocal writing. Over the course of the opera, Mukhtar evolves from an illiterate woman who is unaware of her rights to an advocate for women's education. The vocal writing quite literally mirrors this journey. Though written for coloratura soprano, Mukhtar begins in the middle part of her range. It is only when she decides to defy expectation and assert her autonomy and independence that she moves to the upper, more powerful part of her voice and employing virtuosic coloratura. Thus, the structure of the piece relies as much on the technique of European operatic singing as the structure of Hindustani music.

Like Davis and Huang, I also faced exoticist expectations from the audience in the process of developing *Thumbprint*. For example, one early workshop presentation elicited feedback from White members of the audience indicating that they did not feel the piece was "Indian enough" because it didn't contain "microtones," notwithstanding the fact that the opera is set in Pakistan. One couple went as far as to say that they had expertise in the matter as they had "traveled to India." This feedback early in the developmental process came from an assumption that there is a correct way to portray "South Asian-ness" in a narrative context, and that, even though I am South Asian, I was doing it incorrectly.

This sort of external pressure is problematic not just because it perpetuates musical stereotypes. If the pressure had come from the commissioner instead, it could very well have pushed my compositional approach toward a simulacrum of Indian music rather than allowing me to develop and utilize my own voice as a composer. This exoticist pressure as exerted by gatekeeping forces or society at large can have the additional impact of siloing non-White composers even further: If we write using the techniques of our own cultures, we are deemed "unskilled." But if we don't write "ethnic" music, we are not authentic.

## Conclusion

In discussing my own compositional practice and through conversations with Davis and Huang, I have explored the different ways in which non-White composers approach the musical dramatization of characters long considered Other in the operatic canon. We write with an awareness of our own culture's parallel history of representation in classical music. If we choose to include techniques from this culture, they are not used to denote the culture as Other, but as part of a holistic approach to building character and structure through the entire work. This approach allows for a deeper exploration of the characters themselves and richer, less stereotypical drama. Even so, we continue facing exoticist expectations of the culture around us, including expectations about what the music of a Black or Asian composer "should" sound like. It is my hope that as audiences become more familiar with less exoticized musical dramaturgies of non-White characters, this expectation will lessen and a repertoire that truly represents the global opera community will eventually emerge.

## Notes

1 Ralph P. Locke, "A Broader View of Musical Exoticism," *The Journal of Musicology (St. Joseph, Mich.)* 24, no. 4 (2007): 492.
2 Yayoi Uno Everett, "Intercultural Synthesis in Postwar Western Art Music: Historical Contexts, Perspectives, and Taxonomy," in *Locating East Asia in Western Art Music*, ed. Yayoi Uno Everett and Frederick Lau (Middletown: Wesleyan University Press, 2004), 19.
3 Anthony Davis, in discussion with the author, Zoom, November 2022.
4 In Indian classical music, *Sam* is the beginning and ending of the rhythmic cycle, indicating the cadential return of the rhythmic pattern.
5 Anthony Davis, in discussion with the author, Zoom, November 2022.
6 Ibid.
7 Huang Ruo, in discussion with the author, Bronx, New York, October 2022.
8 Ibid.
9 Ibid.
10 The *rasa* of a raga is its characteristic associated emotional quality.

# 5 Investigating Operatic Decolonization in the Hypermobility Turn

## The Industry's *Sweet Land* (2020)

*Jingyi Zhang*

*Sweet Land* was a site-specific, highly collaborative opera that unfolded as a "grotesque historical pageant."[1] I say "was" to underscore its ontology: it existed and—described by its creators as "an opera that erases itself"—it was an event repeated over a handful of evenings before then disappearing.[2] This opera, produced in Los Angeles at the State Historic Park, uses self-erasure to question colonial histories of the American West and the taking of native lands (the Sweet Land of its title). The opera premiered on 29 February 2020 but closed in early March at the onset of the pandemic. My account is based on a video that was quickly made before the shutdown and attendance at a live performance.[3] While my verb tenses necessarily shift—and I will be referring to an opera (a "work")—the ephemeral reality of the event should not be forgotten.

*Sweet Land* presents alternative, mythologized histories of the encounter between European settlers and the Tongva people, referred to as the "Arrivals" and the "Hosts," respectively, disrupting the static mode of European historical writing. One unconventional feature was the creative team, which was constituted in pairs, with two directors (Yuval Sharon and Cannupa Hanska Luger), two composers (Raven Chacon and Du Yun), and two librettists (Douglas Kearney and Aja Couchois Duncan). Each pair included an Indigenous artist working with opera for the first time, thus offering the creative team the opportunity "to listen to a culture that is not our own," according to Du Yun, which is critical in approaching an opera about settler colonialism.[4] One further unconventional feature was the extremely mobile nature of the performance. Figure 5.1 shows a map illustrating the work of the creative team on both tracks. The event operated simultaneously on two tracks named "Feast" and "Train." Audiences watched the opening "Contact" scene together in an amphitheater. They were then divided into "Feast" or "Train" to watch the first part of their tracks. Next, they headed to an open space for the "Crossroads" scene before returning to the second part of their own tracks. Everyone joined in again in the amphitheater for the coda. The multiple narratives unfolding in time like a vast duet, with voices adjacent to but distant from one another, allude to the violence of colonial displacement.

DOI: 10.4324/9781003462286-8

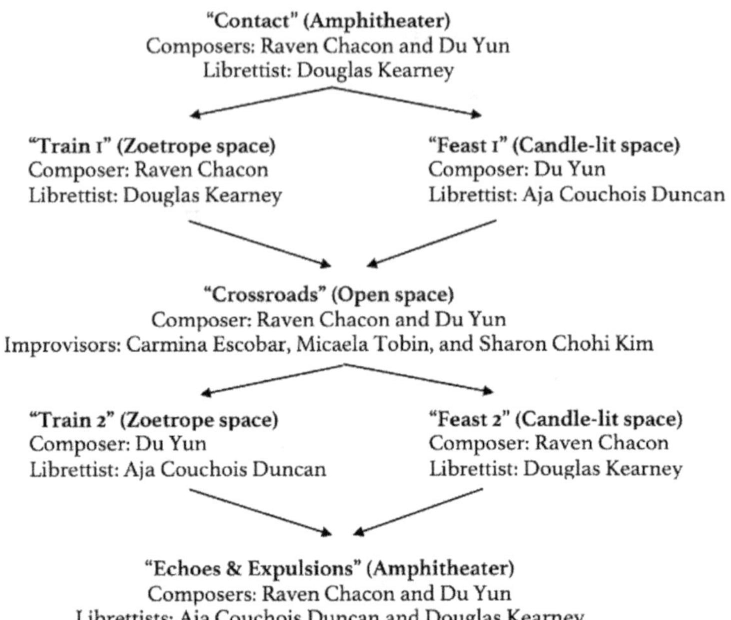


*Figure 5.1* A map showing the logistics for both tracks of the opera, and the work of the creative team.

Besides attending the opera's premiere, I have interviewed Du Yun. My analysis also builds on recent work by Gundula Kreuzer, Jelena Novak, and Megan Steigerwald on site-specific opera and *Sweet Land* in particular.[5] This essay interrogates anew how and whether productions—and events—like *Sweet Land* contribute to operatic decolonization, resisting the generic paradigms of the proscenium stage and its privileged singular perspectives by dislodging audiences from the red velvet seats of the opera house, bewildering them physically, disrupting their ways of knowing a story, and pushing them into subject positions they could not otherwise know. These unanticipated and often disorienting mobilities gesture to what I coin the *hypermobility turn* in opera, a critical framework we can use to examine a new era of operas predicated on breaking barriers and conventions but far beyond more conventional strategies of unsettling, beyond swapping out musical or vocal styles, foregrounding social issues, or choosing an unexpected performance venue. The change is more deep seated. I argue that these alternative and expanded mobilities engaged in and through site-specific performance events like *Sweet Land* carry significant aesthetic, ideological, and ethical ramifications.

## Accusatory Architecture

Let's begin with what might be called the accusatory architecture of *Sweet Land* and its strategies of unsettling. Primal scenes of decolonial thinking were manifested *in* and *through* performances occurring within these structures. "Feast" depicts the "Hosts" feeding the hungry "Arrivals," alluding to the First Thanksgiving. It occurred in a circular structure evoking native American lodges. Audiences were seated in the round, with glowing candles enabling them to see one another clearly throughout, no matter how dark it got. This recalls, in ghostly echo, the social spaces of past European opera, a theater brightly lit, spectators able to see one another across a horseshoe. But this was different: the circular ranks occupied by audiences obviously echoed and extended the circular seating of the "Arrivals" (white settlers) in the operatic fiction before them.

As one fumbled around finding a seat for oneself, crossing in front of fellow attendees, the demographics of audiences was obvious, overwhelmingly echoing the whiteness of the singers playing the "Arrivals." In this mirror-house effect, the (almost exclusively) white settler audiences, who literally *sat with* the "Arrivals," were slotted into visceral identification with settlers and colonizers. "The Arrivals" were, so to speak, an audience as well, gaping at what they witnessed upon their arrival. But they were far from being mere audience; also entering into the spaces they found, becoming characters and agents, changing outcomes, and destroying.

"Train," on the other hand, took place in a towering zoetrope structure and portrayed how the Arrivals industrialized Indigenous knowledge for their own benefit. Zoetrope is one of many 19th-century optical toys that creates the illusion of motion by presenting a series of images inside a revolving cylinder, which spectators view through slits.[6] But here in "Train," the gargantuan zoetrope enclosed spectators, who had to spin around on their swivel chairs to follow the action unfolding behind opening and closing doors. As they rather desperately swiveled around their seats, often trying to search for the singer matching the voice they just heard, interesting things happened. The spectacularization of their own viewing created an intensely embodied perspective: I remember many telegraphing increasing somatic discomfort, as they tried avoiding the gaze of fellow spectators seated nearby.

Let's recall here Michel Foucault's concept of the panopticon: both performance spaces function as what he calls a spontaneous "laboratory of power,"[7] which brings intersectional realities of audiences and people represented by the spectacle to the fore.[8] According to Foucault,

> The panoptic mechanism is not simply a hinge, a point of exchange between a mechanism of power and a function; it is a way of making power relations function in a function, and of making a function function through these power relations.[9]

Foucault's notion that spaces flesh out social contingencies fruitfully resonates with the idea that wide-ranging intersectional realities within audiences (realities like race, ethnicity, and local histories), and the performers they watch, having been carefully positioned within a calculated performance space, nonetheless set in motion spontaneous meaning-making lying beyond the control of the creative team. They made the mix, but how the alchemy worked afterward could not be scripted. Knowledge about colonialism, alertness to mirrorings, shame and individual identities made spectators and listeners into quasi-improvisers and participatory witnesses.

Let's return to "Train" to examine an ideological wrinkle built into the architectural affordances of the panopticon. The setting served as a key media element in the performance, as mentioned earlier: it cultivated an idiosyncratic hyperalertness by forcing you always to shift your gaze. But something was going on beyond delight in optical technology. *This was no toy.* The zoetrope towering over you and the performers sporadically appearing and disappearing behind wooden panels wreak havoc on habits of peaceful viewership. The intense physical and cognitive labor required to follow along obliterated any nostalgic sense that watching opera involves sovereign, immobilized gazing and listening: hyperawareness of one's own body and of labor and disorientation is a recurring theme in audience reactions to *Sweet Land* as shown below:

> "Train" is violent and visceral. Even the set is violent—the wooden panels that make up the round theater slide abruptly on tracks, alternately revealing and concealing the performers in niches behind the audience.
>
> Heidi Waleson, *The Wall Street Journal*

> Despite the ad hoc architecture and the D.I.Y. aesthetic [...] there's a sense of extravagance in the marshaling of dozens of artists and so many technical challenges for something that passes so quickly.
>
> Zachary Woolfe, *The New York Times*

> the rolling walls that serve as evocations of locomotives in "Train" [...] is a remarkable feat of design—like being placed in a swirling vortex.
>
> Carolina Miranda, *Los Angeles Times*

With these shifting optical mobilities, the upending, ideally, produced not just a certain keenness in perception but *an understanding.*[10] The process of being tossed into and caught up in the optical play before them invited audiences to recognize and reflect on the complicated—and problematic—nature of seeing and the accountability of the seeing subject.

Expanding the notion of site-specific operas, one notices that it's not merely the alternative site itself which shakes things up, creates novelty for the jaded. Alternative sites can steer transactions occurring *within* and *among* spectators and listeners, generating ephemeral and unexpected experiential orders emerging in the here-and-now.[11] These highly specific, deceptively minuscule, and completely spontaneous mobilities, which harbor intense ideological implications for audience members during a performance event, demonstrate a new ethos and political sensibility embraced by the *hypermobility turn* in contemporary operas today.

## On Representation and Representability

But while indicating dynamism, the *hypermobility turn* also carries with it a sense of breathlessness underlying the compulsion to decolonize opera. New questions are raised about complicity and whether its utopian aspirations were cross-talked by the creators' own decisions about depiction and representation. Thus, let's interrogate some casting decisions. The racially diverse creative team and cast wielded significant agency. But here comes something that's more difficult to disentangle: did that change anything? Despite the progressive rhetoric surrounding the production, I argue that the resistance ***to*** Indigenous stereotypes does not debunk the stereotypes, so much as it signals the impossibility of imagining ***otherwise***. Even with a creative team and cast that consist mainly of members of historically underrepresented communities, the multiethnic production could still end up reinscribing the same essentialist impulse it intended to escape from in their compulsion for new versions of objectification.

Casting *any* non-white member as *any* Indigenous character casually erased any nuances, any reality of race. The flattening of identities thus points to an unnerving truth: the crave for representation is so deeply embedded in the *skin* of the production that it does not matter who play "the Hosts," as long as they make up a sea of non-whiteness. Diversity has become an end unto itself. Having a Black, Indigenous, and person of color (BIPOC) with vastly different stories, traditions, and cultural touchstones from an Indigenous member to serve as spokesperson for the Indigenous community further falls prey to what philosopher Olúfemi Táíwò calls "elite capture,"[12] in which *already* privileged individuals merely "*cosmetically* elevate"[13] Indigenous voices.

Fred Moten critiques exhaustive attempts at defining and ontologizing the non-white subject, viewing them as falling back into the same essentializing traps seen in both anti-Blackness discourses *and* discourses that celebrate Blackness.[14] Echoing Moten, Girim Jung asserts, "Anti-blackness therefore can be reproduced in mundane scenes of black performativity."[15] Likewise, in *Sweet Land*, having a majority of non-white performers could *still* paradoxically perpetuate anti-Indigenous essentialisms.

This paradoxical phenomenon is symptomatic of the decolonial compulsion driving much of today's contemporary productions. To illustrate, let's make a brief but necessary detour to another opera conceived in the *hypermobility turn*, Yuval Sharon's *Twilight: Gods*, which presents radical reimaginations of Richard Wagner's *Götterdämmerung* in parking garages in Detroit and Chicago. The collaboration with historically underrepresented artists, inclusive casting practices, and musical crossover efforts might, at first blush, seem like a socially progressive act. But one must be mindful of such displays of equality and not embrace the sharing of space—optically and musically speaking—as an automatic signifier of "progressiveness." Although there was a scene ("Siegfried's Funeral March") that taps into legendary Black music of the 1960s, reducing it to audible stereotypes of Motown deprived a more meaningful engagement with Black musicality. Moreover, the episode had no bearing on the characters or drama beyond mere intention to *display* Black musical tradition, hence striking one as simplistic. The instantaneous transition to Motown from Wagner's music that came before demonstrates no attempt to transform, unsettle, or destabilize the original music. What we heard was a convenient *merger* between Wagner and Motown, each musical element kept unchanged and separate from each other. A musical collaboration premised on "fitting" Black music into the dominant Western paradigm perpetuates a new form of musical essentialism resembling the reductive flattening of identities as discussed in *Sweet Land.* The way to characterize such decolonial moves is like pouring old wine into new bottle. The wine has not been changed, just what bottle, and who is doing the pouring.

But the larger issue at stake here concerns *representability*. There was a striking scene in the first part of "Feast" in *Sweet Land* when the Indigenous protagonist, Makwa introduced herself to the "Arrivals" through a brief dance. Her dance moves are hard-edged and the accompaniment is more EDM than traditional song. Her wordless vocalization on "ah" embellished with sharp vibratos further distinguished her from other characters. The same electronic beats, melismas, and kungfu moves reappeared the next time she sang. The unconventional portrayals upended stereotypical perceptions of Indigeneity but we wonder: if an Indigenous performance departs significantly from what settler audiences presume to be authentic, is the new portrayal automatically radical, and therefore progressive?

True enough, the *alternative* representation deprived audiences of what Dylan Robinson calls "settler hunger," the quick satiation of one's desire for familiarity.[16] But it gave mixed signals. It's saying, how different. But it's also declaring, what a spectacle! The problematic issue of *representability* enters. I'd suggest that departing from exotic markers did *not* make Makwa's dance any *less* exotic. In fact, wordless vocalization continues to perpetuate exotic associations. We heard new idiosyncrasies like big vocal leaps, chromaticisms, and syncopations sung in 11/16. Projecting an opposite—but equally hypervisible/audible—Makwa would only create *another* Single Exotic Other after all, which presumes *knowability* of the Other, and effortless, unmediated access to Indigenous representability. To preserve the subject's unknowability, it is valuable to turn to Édouard Glissant's idea of "opacity," which frustrates clear interpretation.[17]

The persistence of unknowability—alluding to a multiplicity of subjectivities—respects the irreducibility of the subject, thus enabling "new pathways" of understandings to emerge.[18] This is acquired first by acknowledging the fundamental impossibility of knowing the Other, which gestures to a kind of striving—or "point[ing] towards" as Moten suggested—in contemporary operas' ongoing efforts at decolonization.[19]

"Point[ing] towards" implies that the goal cannot be reached and it is striving toward it that counts, which raises problematic questions about access to Indigenous epistemologies, particularly how does one represent Indigenous culture, what an opera that subverts nothing, adopts fresh angles, and just *be* (i.e., free from decolonial compulsion) look and sound like, and how does one get to this alternative place of seeing, feeling, and doing. Carolyn Abbate is reckoning with the fundamental impossibility of arriving at this alternative place. In comments during a recent conference on Vernacular Philosophy, she suggested the following:

> There's a compulsion to try knowing that futility is immanent in the effort. This is a really important idea and that is the way to put it. You try, knowing that futility is built into the effort. [...] But how are we sure that we can get to this alternative place [...]? We know that we have to listen attentively, and be willing to undertake this labor. Practise in the knowledge that the hoped-for benefit is going to remain unattainable.[20]

## Phantasmagoria and Aporia

*Sweet Land*'s coda, "Echoes & Expulsions," offered a provocative glimpse of a kind of striving in the radical experimentation with hypermediality, engendering an immense, aesthetic surplus through the various media, voices, and texts at play, leading to ex-centric forms of knowing. Audiences returned to the dark amphitheater and were greeted by a media-saturated fable: all scrims were removed, revealing a lone child laboring in the open wasteland, as shown in Figure 5.2 below. He vocalized mournfully on "woo," later joined in by four overlapping amplified acousmatic voices, accompanied by unseen instrumentalists from afar, holograms of galloping horses (a classic zoetrope theme), and the LA Metro. Surtitles drawing on real stories of colonial violence were projected everywhere.

Phantasmagoric excess pervaded this everyday sight, rendering the city deeply uncanny. As asserted by Azania Khatri-Patel, cities are "fertile grounds for hauntings" shaped by caged routines, body-less voices, and cold machinery.[21] This final scene of ghosting—disembodied voices emerging from nowhere, misbehaving texts escaping from LED screens, and empty metro-automatons chugging on—occupied a parallel universe governed by its own laws. We were plunged into a nightmare reality of our own making: a hyper-technologized netherworld where every human encounter was mediated by an invisible technological ghost, leading us to question whether *we* have finally become ghosts in the machine and how an opera can represent all of this.

*Figure 5.2* "Echoes & Expulsions" scene of phantasmagoria. ©Casey Kringlen and Neil Matsumoto.

Referring to the coda as "a phoenix moment," Du Yun remarked the following in our interview:

> We didn't want to be confined to the story of Makwa, Jimmy Gin, Preacher, we wanted to open up […] to one's reverberation and memory. So, at the end, it's like, let's forget about opera, because this is happening right now, in this moment. And that's why when you hear the train, the helicopter, these objects are "activated" by you. […] for me, it's so interesting to *not* follow the characters. You just activate your imagination and only hear the voices, ghost memory, and the morsel of your cultural memory. That, to me, is so powerful.[22]

Evidently, she was skeptical of opera's efficacy in coming to terms with something that's unfolding still. The enigmatic portrayal of opera disappearing into life was a point-blank recognition of opera's incapacity to represent the ongoingness of colonial encroachment in the everyday.

Finally, it is worth reflecting on the absence of a proper ontological closure, which reaches beyond an operatic *cannot* in envoicing an ethical aporia—a reflex of colonial shame perhaps. Or rather, a communal aporia, which speaks to a certain humility on the part of the creative team in asking: who are we to think that we can represent these people and their lives and their stories? Or is this a poetic aporia for no opera could ever attempt to redress historical wrongs? Maybe even a traumatic aporia so radical that opera itself is called into question. And self-erasure is a way—perhaps the only way—to record, and make space for the unsayable, leaving many audiences in doubt about the propriety of clapping at the end. Because opera, at this point, is a simple epiphenomenon.

## Decolonization and Epistemic Humility

This series of cannots gestures to the notion of epistemic humility. The conundrum thus stands: what is the value of humility, and what would true fidelity to humility entail? While working with epistemic humility, how do we prevent ourselves from getting entrapped in yet another ontological claim or novel dictum, albeit set against western frameworks? Perhaps thinking with humility as part of our epistemological framework in our ongoing path to decolonize can inspire one to dedicate oneself to unspectacular moments that might otherwise escape the purview of what most deem worthy of attention. And they can encompass many things, ranging from improvisatory musical styles to the kind of asymptotic striving observed in *Sweet Land*'s coda, which paradoxically gestures to the ultimate futility of representability itself. These moments depart from our conventional but unquestioned adulation of only monumental works that promises to transform.

But above all, we must learn to sit with the unknowable and just *be*. This does not mean surrendering in the face of futility. On the contrary, we must embrace an epistemic openness all the more so, and demonstrate genuine capaciousness in our decolonial thinking. For even if we fail, our ongoing struggle can generate unexpected gains and epiphanies, which in themselves justify continued striving, and may open the gateway to a *captureless* (hence more hopeful) future.

## Notes

1 The Industry, "Production: *Sweet Land*," accessed September 2, 2021, https://theindustryla.org/projects/sweet-land/.

2 Ibid.

3 The opera was quickly videotaped with creative nimbleness, if not elite production values, before the shutdown. More in *Sweet Land: A New Opera by The Industry*, Vimeo (Los Angeles State Historic Park, 2020), http://stream.sweetlandopera.com.

4 Joshua Barone, "An Opera About Colonialism Shows How History Warps," The New York Times, February 28, 2020, sec. Music, https://www.nytimes.com/2020/02/28/arts/music/sweet-land-opera.html?searchResultPosition=2.

5 Gundula Kreuzer, "Butterflies on Sweet Land? Reflections on Opera at the Edges of History," *Representations* 154, no. 1 (2021): 69–86; Megan Steigerwald Ille, "'No Sweet Land Here:' Spectating Erasure in The Industry's Sweet Land," in *Session 6a: Community and Collaboration* (47th Annual Conference of the Society for American Music, virtual, 2021); Megan Steigerwald Ille, "The Operatic Ear: Mediating Aurality," *Sound Stage Screen* 1, no. 1 (Spring 2021): 119–43; Megan Steigerwald Ille, "Live in the Limo: Remediating Voice and Performing Spectatorship in Twenty-First-Century Opera," *The Opera Quarterly* 36, no. 1 (2021): 1–26; Jelena Novak, "*Sweet Land*, a New Opera by The Industry," *Sound Stage Screen* 1, no. 1 (Spring 2021): 275–83.

6 Sharon himself described the zoetrope effect as a "flipbook," where static images viewed in quick succession created an illusion of motion, echoing the Enlightenment myth of progress lying at the heart of the opera. See James C. Taylor, "Yuval Sharon Reinvents Opera for Los Angeles," *Los Angeles Review of Books*, March 28, 2020, https://lareviewofbooks.org/article/yuval-sharon-reinvents-opera-for-los-angeles/;

Meghan Perkins, "Two Different Stories, Two Different Sets in *Sweet Land*," *Live Design*, April 13, 2020, https://www.livedesignonline.com/theatre/two-different-stories-two-different-sets-sweet-land.

7 Michel Foucault, "Panopticism," in *Discipline and Punish: The Birth of the Prison*, 2nd Vintage Books ed. (New York: Vintage Books, 1995), 204.

8 Foucault, 204.

9 Foucault, 206–7.

10 This resonates with media archaeologist Wanda Strauven who asserted that the zoetrope spectators were transformed "more consciously into […] perception makers" in the process. More in Wanda Strauven, "The Observer's Dilemma: To Touch or Not to Touch," in *Media Archaeology: Approaches, Applications, and Implications*, ed. Erkki Huhtamo and Jussi Parikka (Berkeley: University of California Press, 2019), 150, 154.

11 This logic is also at work in Martha Feldman's "Magic Mirrors and the Seria Stage: Thoughts toward a Ritual View" where she challenges the fixedness of an opera seria performance by discussing the divergent meanings engendered by the performance, which are consolidated by local audiences. More specifically, she argued that modes of production converge with local histories, political contexts, and experiential conditions across time to "make seria many things to many people." More in Martha Feldman, "Magic Mirrors and the Seria Stage: Thoughts toward a Ritual View," *Journal of the American Musicological Society* 48, no. 3 (1995): 426.

12 More on the concept of "elite capture" in Olúfẹmi O. Táíwò, *Elite Capture: How the Powerful Took over Identity Politics (and Everything Else)* (Chicago: Haymarket Books, 2022).

13 Olúfẹmi O. Táíwò, "Being in the Room," in *Elite Capture: How the Powerful Took over Identity Politics (and Everything Else)* (Chicago: Haymarket Books, 2022), 83.

14 More in Fred Moten, *Black and Blur* (Durham: Duke University Press, 2017). Girim Jung, echoing Fred Moten, posits that "Blackness is not a definitive singularity but pluriform, implying entanglement and haunting doublings between seemingly paradoxical aspects in dialectical tension that blur or destabilize established categories and definitions." See Girim Jung, "Resisting Ontologization: An Intercultural Comparison of Glissant, Moten, and Suh," *Journal of World Philosophies* 5 (Summer 2020): 253.

15 Jung, "Resisting Ontologization: An Intercultural Comparison of Glissant, Moten, and Suh," 246.

16 Dylan Robinson, "Hungry Listening," in *Hungry Listening: Resonant Theory for Indigenous Sound Studies* (Minneapolis: University of Minnesota Press, 2020), 49.

17 Jung, 244. Kwami Coleman further engaged with Édouard Glissant's idea of "opacity," viewing it as a fundamental human right to not be fully known and understood, not to be totally legible and understandable. He elaborated that a subject should at all times resist an interrogative gaze and complete knowability. More in Kwami Coleman, "Panel Discussion" (University of Oxford (Vernacular Philosophies of Music Symposium, virtual), 2022).

18 Jung, "Resisting Ontologization: An Intercultural Comparison of Glissant, Moten, and Suh," 244.

19 Jung, 249.

20 Carolyn Abbate, "Lightness, Efficacy, Unknowability" (Vernacular Philosophies of Music Symposium, University of Oxford (virtual), 2022).

21 Azania Imtiaz Khatri-Patel, "The Haunted City," *Aeon*, June 28, 2022, https://aeon.co/essays/ghosts-haunt-cities-seeking-revenge-for-the-disappeared-past.

22 Yun Du, Interview with Du Yun about The Industry's *Sweet Land* (2020), interview by Jingyi Zhang, August 11, 2022.

# 6 Interview with Du Yun

*Du Yun and Jingyi Zhang*

*JZ:* It's truly a great experience attending *Sweet Land*'s community preview before the shutdown in March. How was the opera conceived initially? Did the performance space (LA State Historic Park) play a significant role in shaping your compositional language? Could you share with us how you wove in site-related considerations into your composition, metaphorically and materially?

*DY:* Sure. When we conceived the work, we didn't talk about who the characters are. We know that we want to make a work reflective of our collective memory and frustration but also using that as an entry point to the freedom of not abiding by any storylines. We also had this idea of having parallel storylines that speak to our own realities and that's the erasure. We also talked about eraser, erased histories which came up repeatedly in our early meetings, and this brutal reality that we're living in.

And then, we ask ourselves, how can we make all this work into a singular experience? Then, we're looking at structure, which is both form and architectural structure. Site is not just a venue but also its shape and frame. It gradually became clear that we wanted to have two circular structures. At one point, we even talked about having a horse! Obviously, we're not going to have a horse, but it's an important idea of the interstitial, which was what "Crossroads" was about. So, little by little, when you're digging away, before you even know it, you actually see the structure of the work.

We're then also looking at possibilities of performance site and we eventually decided on the historical park, which was a very happy result. There are other sites that we were also very excited about, but the Los Angeles State Historic Park feels very appropriate because it was also nicknamed "the cornfields." And considering its close proximity to Chinatown, we cannot *not* talk about Chinese labor if you're looking at US history, so I really wanted to pay tribute to the site. But we also don't want to resort to essentializations of immigrant histories. We did more research and discovered that the 1888 Chinatown

DOI: 10.4324/9781003462286-9

Massacre occurred in Los Angeles, and this important history contributed to the depth of this work.

We also talked about many different awful things that could happen in the middle, but gradually we realized that it's going to happen in the final scene when things are things, and the site becomes the character itself when the scrim is unveiled for the first time. You see the projection on the highway, and the billboard, a little boy, and two Coyotes far away.

The coda was, to me, one of the most personal and touching moments, especially when you're *not* seeing Makwa, Preacher, etc. but you're actually thinking about yourself and your ancestors. And the land that we're seeing and hearing the music in is vibrating with cultural memories. The land itself becomes more than a character, more than a site to put your work on, but is pregnant with all those threads.

*JZ:* The paired collaboration concept is very innovative. Could you talk more about the collaborative dynamic? How did the creatives work with the co-directors Yuval Sharon and Cannupa Hanska Luger? Did the performers play a role in the creative process?

*DY:* Dramaturgically, I think we're all there contributing to ideas collectively. I do very much like the paired collaboration concept, where there is one Native American creative in each pair. I would also work out many things with Aja Couchois Duncan since the musical beats also determined many dramatic elements. Though there was no dramaturg, we talked about dramaturgy together. It was helpful to have Elizabeth, the executive director, in the room asking questions since she has a visual arts background. We all talked about motivations, structure, duration, and do bear in mind, this opera is not Yuval's culture, so that's when he realized he needed another director, and we got connected with Cannupa who is a genius slash engineer. Yuval really loved Cannupa's ideas and asked him to serve as co-director. I think it's an astute decision because *Sweet Land* is a work that subverts dominant narratives, so it makes sense to have a real double team where everyone's listening attentively to each other. Obviously, there are differences in approach, but we generate ideas collectively, and we're always together in the room.

Cannupa is so visionary and piercing, so though he had never directed an opera before, he brought with him so many ideas, concepts, and criticisms that blew my mind. Cannupa is also very vested in technology. Native Americans have their own technology that's inherently associated with the social function of each character manifested in his/her/their look, costume, and emotional state. Cannupa was so piercingly accurate on all these fronts.

Performers do play a key role in artistic decisions. Coyotes were so much about Carmina Escobar and Micaela Tobin, and the Windigo, Sharon Chohi Kim. This trio was amazing! They came up with the idea of the "Crossroads" scene where they engaged in this virtuosic performance of voices. Another instance took place one day when Carmina wanted to make a track together. Janine Washington came in and began to sing a song from her tribe, which I just fell in love with. And we spent some time in the recording studio and came up with something which now becomes the first track you hear in our album.

*JZ:* Could you share with us how the different operatic characters in *Sweet Land* came about? And how did you compose music for these characters?

*DY:* Windigo and Coyote belong to Native American literature, so we had to do our research on these characters and ask ourselves many questions when composing for these characters. And the character Grandpa was about offerings and paying respect to the land, so we must think about land connection, ideas of migration, etc., which drove me to adopt a mix between metal music and Mongolian music. When he was saying here's the land and here're some food and offering, I started hearing those Mongolian long songs. But I don't resort to musical essentializations. Raven would have remarked, why would *any* tribe be the spokesperson for *all* tribes, right? By drawing on Mongolian musical influences, I'm not saying that Native Americans walked from Asia, I'm just implying that it *could* all be happening. That's a very long migration! Raven is very interested in that idea too. We were both musing over the possibility of what if they walked back to Asia? We had a good laugh about it. Now you can see, no one was serious about origin. It's about the spirit that matters.

*JZ:* It's so fabulous that both Raven Chacon and you are Pulitzer Prize winners! Could you speak more about the process of composing with Chacon whom I understand was working in opera for the first time? How did the compositional aspect of this collaboration work out?

*DY:* Raven and I are both performers which help us understand the dramaturgical aspects of the opera. I have also performed together with him. In both performance and dramaturgy, you're using the same mechanism and muscles because you're listening intently with each other, and adapting very quickly in the here-and-now. Same goes for composing. And Raven is one of those really thoughtful artists, so both of us—together with everyone on the creative team—talk about dramaturgy.

*JZ:* The character of Jimmy Gin is really striking. He's played by a countertenor, sings and acts in an exaggerated, flamboyant way, so it's clearly a *marked* role. The music that accompanies him harks back to an archaic style that's connected to Handel operas and the castrato figure. But on the other hand, it's participating in a recent genealogy in contemporary operas, and I'm thinking of Nico Muhly's *Marnie*, Thomas Ades' *The Exterminating Angel*, and John Corigliano's *The Lord of Cries*, where there's this otherworldliness, sinisterness that's built into this countertenor role (i.e., Terry, Francisco, and Dionysus). Could you share with us how it was like writing for Jimmy Gin? Were his exaggerated vocal flourishes meant as a kind of critique of the western tradition at large?

*DY:* I've always had a fixation on the gay cowboy character, which was why I wrote for a countertenor. I had this idea of a closeted, emasculated gay figure who doesn't fit in his society and wants to take everything. I know many people will associate the countertenor voice with Baroque music, but that was contemporary music back in the 17th century. In a sense, he's bringing "contemporary" music with him onto the ship and he encounters Makwa who belongs to another futuristic, imaginary world. For me at least, it's about seeing these two parallel streams of contemporary music happening together at once, colliding into each other, which is a more interesting thought. A lot of people including our own Douglas Kearney perceive Jimmy Gin's voice as performing some kind of criticism of the western tradition at large. I don't hear it as criticism at all. I think that we always listen with our own lens. True enough, he was funny, but that's him. I approach this character directly and never intended him or his voice to perform any kind of criticism.

Sometimes when scholars think and write academically, they're removing all these *other* layers from a character. There are so many emotional layers in a character that defeat categorization and render words futile, which is precisely what drives me to make music, and take on an opera like this. And scholars often tend to approach a work like a detective, trying to seek for underlying "meanings," which I find problematic. I think that they are at once over-reading and not reading enough. It would be so much easier to write parody music for Jimmy Gin than to actually consider him as a modern character who's performing this parallel idea with Makwa because that, to me, is a much more brutal reality. When you're saying that Jimmy Gin is making fun of the western tradition, you're already putting yourself in a static position. If, however, you're actually encountering him as a fresh character, something that's happening in the here-and-now, you'll appreciate the many beautiful lines in his singing. It's like throwing the blanket into the air and let that be. To me, as a creative, that's much messier and that's the place I want to be.

*JZ:* I'm also struck by the character of Makwa, and her dance scene, which was very brief and unconventional, especially when we compare it with other operas with Indigenous characters. Makwa's dance was hard-edged, not alluring, and she's not accompanied by traditional Indigenous instruments but cymbals, electronic sounds, and booming static noises. Could you comment on how you approached this character?

*DY:* Makwa is futuristic. Music-wise, I was hearing this Sri Lankan, British artist, M.I.A. whose "Paper Planes" captures Makwa's energy, so I modeled Makwa on M.I.A. Don't ask me why. It was very important for Makwa to be futuristic, electronic, and fearless, so the electronic beats are fitting of her character. But she must start off with the impression that she's the future of the land. Makwa is about the spirit to me.

And her dance moves weren't in the libretto. I just had this idea that it's going to be very kung fu-like but not Chinese kung fu. She has to *present* herself. Cannupa talked a lot about the social function aspect in Native American culture—if you're a bowl, you don't use a bowl, you actually *are* a bowl, you *are* a knife, etc. So, if you are something, you *are* something. I felt that the presentation is so important, which is also true in kung fu. So Makwa can't just speak. She must *present* herself.

One big issue I have with traditional opera is that the characters *always* sing. But when you see good acting in contemporary operas and films, the performers don't just deliver nice cheap college plays, but they are so immersed in what they're doing and you see their eyes and hand gestures do something. If they're angry, they don't yell but do something so completely and amazingly different from what you would expect which blows your mind. That's always something that speaks to me. Singers don't always have to sing, especially when a very important character has come in or a very important emotion is unfolding. Those are the moments I always take great care with.

*JZ:* Could you comment on the finale of *Sweet Land*, a very haunting ending with voices coming from nowhere, surtitles escaping from LED screens, and the metro that passes by every few minutes, intruding on the performance. What were some of the conversations the creative team had about this final scene? Given all this excess in media, is there a particular message intended to be conveyed?

*DY:* It's so clear that in the coda, we wanted to open up to our current brutal reality. It's very interesting because for future iterations of this finale, we always talk about how this structure could offer a different approach to each specific land. So, the finale is a collection of seven to nine short songs. We've also thought about having this in the middle but then it was at the end. And then we chose four stories that connected to us the most, and I feel that I have to write about the Chinatown massacre—it's part of my social responsibility. And there are moments like Rosa (a young Pomo girl of age ten) who sings "No Sweet Land here. No Sweet Land here." It's the best line I've ever written. I have to say it was so good. It just feels so right.

We did not want to be confined to the story of Makwa, Jimmy Gin, the train, Preacher, Scribe, Bow, the horse, etc. but we wanted to get back to one's reverberation and memory. If you're an immigrant, you always know how complex that story could be. For me, the final scene was the most successful part of the opera when all of a sudden, this manmade structure is unveiled. So at the end, it's like, let's forget about opera, because this is happening right now, in this moment. And that's why when you hear the train, the helicopter, these objects are "activated" by you. But so is life. And I think for me, it's so interesting to *not* follow the characters. You just activate your imagination and hear the voices, ghost memory, and morsel of your cultural memory. That, to me, is so powerful. And that's why the overlapping voices work. It makes sense, musically and conceptually. And this was a phoenix moment for me too, because so many deaths have happened in both tracks. "Train 2" was a burned down, dystopic ending. "Feast 2" was deliberately made very bare, very economical, and really heartbreaking in a beautiful way. But despite ending so differently music-wise, both tracks gesture to the idea that there's nowhere to go. Then, you must have that release which really worked successfully.

*JZ:* If there's one thing you could have done differently, what would that be, if any?

*DY:* I think we all wanted to redo the opening scene. We're not deleting it, because that also removes the power of coming back at the end. I just don't think we need all those characters in the beginning and must rethink how to introduce these characters. It's a little confusing for audiences. To me, the introduction needs to be much faster and more open. But for a world premiere production, what we came up with in 2020 was truly good. But if we were to remount it someday, we would rethink not just musically but also in terms of text, story, and staging. Perhaps we can set it as a school play which is typical of how American history is learnt or it could be a funny situation. And perhaps not stage it in that epic way but in a different site that's more bare. I'm very interested in seeing how this remount is going to work if there're no structures like that. For someone like you who have seen the live performance, you might like that better because there's so much activeness on the audiences' part. But most people haven't experienced that live. We have seen some really interesting sites, which could lead to many amazing possibilities. I'm confident that we can make it so much better!

*JZ:* Does your identity—as a Chinese-American woman in the 21st-century America—consciously impact your compositional practice and the stories you choose to tell? Do you feel a sense of responsibility to tell particular stories today in a particular way?

*DY:* Yes and no. I hear these questions a lot. I think as an artist, you always change, with time and age. When I was a teenager, I was only concerned about saving Chinese culture. It was my mission back then. And of course, when you grow older, you discard all those rigid thinking, and you just want to be you and make a name for yourself that people can remember you by. I'm also a performer, so I do so many different exciting things. And before you know, ten years have passed, and you have a body of works that already *becomes* who you are. And I gradually realized that I will let my body of work speak for itself, and people can throw whatever labels they want on me. I don't want to define myself; it's not my job to do their job. Their job might be to define, and I'm not going to spend my time to help them define me. My job is to create a body of works, which will redefine their ideas. Even if I try communicating with them about my ideas, they will still put you in a box! Genre-defying is still a genre in itself.

Let me put it in more concrete terms. You cannot escape your own life experiences, no matter what musical concepts you're using or who you think you are. When zoom is malfunctioning, when your laptop is turned off, when I'm walking down the streets, people perceive me only within three seconds of judgment as a five-feet, short Chinese woman. And that becomes part of your life experience. How people treat you based on this judgment also forms part of your life experience. Your worldview, values, and ideas are constantly informed by your life experiences which you cannot escape from. This is different from saying that I feel socially responsible because once you put yourself in the role of a Messiah, it can be very dangerous, so I try not to do that. But I like to think of myself as a mediator.

But having just a progressive attitude is not right either. It's so easy to talk about hashtag, make space for members of historically marginalized communities, sure, but the current "woke" phenomenon is very narrow-minded because it's not led by the right people. People whom you're trying to decolonize don't care about everything you say. All those things said about decolonization is to make the speaker feel better, but let's do real work and really look at how much funding and (creative) resources are going back to the ground, and to those people. That's what I'm worried about. Don't talk to me about lofty, artistic ideas; let's talk about money. When you do fundraising, make sure that's your top one priority. Don't talk about making space for BIPOC without trying to pay them well. That's why when I have a band, my first priority is always to pay them well.

I'm not whining. I'm one of those luckiest people with resources, which is why I want to share them with others and work even harder to continue making that possible. And that's not to say that I'm pressurized to feel this responsibility, but it's about being aware that I have so much power thinking about wild ideas and making them happen. How many people in the world can say that's happening to them? So few, and so exceptional, right? So precisely because I feel so lucky and indebted, that I want to be responsible rather than sit around and do nothing.

That's what motivated my Future Tradition initiative because so many regional operas are being viewed as "world music," which completely blows my mind. I want to do projects that collaborate with musicians who come from oral traditions but lack the access and skills to collaborate. That's where I want to make space for them. There're lots to experiment with, and rethink how improvisation works, and how to collaborate with people from oral and folk traditions. How do we negotiate with these languages? That's also something that composers and creatives absolutely and desperately need to have. And that's not because I feel the responsibility to do these things. As Cannupa said which I'm now sharing with you, I think we should think less about taking responsibility; it's about accountability. I'm willing to keep moving forward and always make myself accountable, but I should not feel that I have the responsibility. When I curate, I don't do it because I feel the responsibility to do that. It's so unfair that it's the so-called under-represented who feel the responsibility.

*JZ:* What is your view on decolonization in opera?

*DY:* I've been to so many panels on decolonization and issues of indigeneity in opera, etc. I think that decolonization is such a loose term. There's an excess of anger but a lack of why and how. With Raven, Cannupa, and Aja, it's incredible that there was never really any anger. There are many times I've been to a room where I'm not allowed to touch anything. With our Native creatives, there was no anger but a lot of pushbacks. There's always why, followed by very articulated, piercing thinking that goes right into your heart, which tattoos your vision in a particular way. And you use that thinking or approach in so many other things as well. That, to me, is very powerful.

# Part III

# Site-Specific Dramaturgies

# 7 Landscape Dramaturgy and (Post)Opera

## Singing after Perspective[1]

*Jelena Novak*

This text was inspired by a series of fluid encounters with displaced and borderline moments of singing, both within the realm of (post)opera and beyond.[2] These encounters include a lake, skater, and "singing ice" captured on the outskirts of Stockholm and featured respectively in the 2018 National Geographic documentary video "Hear the Otherworldly Sounds of Skating on Thin Ice"[3]; the operatic staging of Hans Werner Henze's 1971 oratorio *Das Floß der Medusa* ("The Raft of the Medusa"), directed by Romeo Castellucci in 2018 at the Dutch National Opera[4]; and the silent "floating voice" in Julie Gautier's 2018 short underwater film *Ama*.[5]

All of them are connected to waterscapes and the altering of one's perception of breathing, moving, walking, singing, and living in water (including ice). These moments of singing while the protagonist is submerged, swimming, or skating create situations that challenge conventions of terrestrial life and gravitational laws that we often take for granted, like breathing air, the bodily balance involved in walking on a solid surface, and perspectival viewing. The nature of vocal performance is transformed in these instances. The following questions arise: Can an inanimate, unbreathing element like ice produce song? How is that song being perceived? How is singing related to swimming and drowning ("The Raft of the Medusa")? Is it possible to produce the voice underwater (*Ama*)?

While only Castellucci's staging occurs in the (post)operatic context, I deem all three examples pertinent to the inquiry of postoperatic singing. The singing ice and underwater voice represent idiosyncratic performance moments somewhat close to "artless singing," which reveal a critical change in perspective and perception of the singing voice.[6] The former unfolds entirely outside artistic institutions in nature, while the latter occurs underwater in freediving choreography, which serves as the backdrop for an underwater silent film captured in the Y-40 Deep Joy swimming pool.

In addition to these unconventional vocal performances, I draw inspiration from several texts and contexts revolving around encounters with perspective

DOI: 10.4324/9781003462286-11

and landscape as posited by Ana Vujanović,[7] Wolfgang Ernst's conception of sonicity,[8] and the relationality between human voice and the hiss of the turtle in an attempt to propose a definition of posthuman voice.[9] Ultimately, I find elements of landscape dramaturgy, as defined by Vujanović, woven into all of these experiences.

In her diptych of texts on landscape dramaturgy, Vujanović, on the one hand, questions conventional notions of landscape in which the land is staged for the viewer as scenery, and on the other, the concept of perspective as a model of thought, visual technique, and method of representing space on a surface. Perspective theory was devised in the early fifteenth-century by the Italian architect Filippo Brunelleschi and systematized by Leon Battista Alberti in his 1435 treatise *Della pittura* ("On Painting"). Vujanović writes, "In the field of performing arts, the perspective doesn't only address set design… perspective operates conceptually, helping us to organize visual experience of performance."[10] Quoting Sergej Pristaš, Vujanović posits,

> even when we don't have the perspectival set design, the logic of perspective influences how we usually organize the space by attaching more attention and importance to the actions upfront, while those in background are often counter-actions, lateral events, latent streams, or additional information about the main action.[11]

How does perspective influence the (post)operatic listening experience? For instance, how does the concept of perspective (and beyond) shape one's perception of the singing voice? While commenting on the distinctions between film and opera, librettist Royce Vavrek draws on the operatic adaptation of Lars von Trier's *Melancholia* (2011) to highlight the impact of perspective:

> One difference is that filmed media has the advantage of the close-up: a camera can fix itself on an actor's face and communicate the most intimate sentiments of that character's experience. In opera, the close-up is the aria, often an inner monologue that exposes the character's current emotional condition, or their psychology working through a complex process.[12]

The cultivation of multiple perspectives and shared viewpoints constitute crucial tools in landscape dramaturgy, as discussed by Vujanović. In what follows, I examine the conceptual framework of landscape dramaturgy as manifested in key instances of singing within and around postopera—both artistic and artless—accounting for not only the visual but also the aural, and for desynchronization between what is seen and what is heard at the same time while the singing takes place.

## Waterscape: The Singing Ice

The National Geographic video "Hear the Otherworldly Sounds of Skating on Thin Ice" captures the ice of the frozen lake in Sweden as it "sings." The description states:

> The small lake outside Stockholm emits otherworldly sounds as Mårten Ajne skates over its precariously thin, black ice. "Wild ice skating" or "Nordic skating" is both an art and a science. A skater seeks out the thinnest, most pristine black ice possible—both for its smoothness, and for its high-pitched, laser-like sounds.[13]

Otherworldly here obviously refers to the non-human. In an interview with Amy Rankin, Ajne explains why the black ice is good at singing:

> In the video, the sounds are created by me skating on it. There is a distinctive sonorous tone and the noise from cracks striking. [...] The sonorous tone is the song of black ice, best heard (and recorded) from a short distance. The layman explanation would be that the tone is inversely related to the thickness of the ice. The thinner the ice, the higher the tone. Intriguingly, the ice is about to collapse at high C, the supposedly highest note of a soprano opera singer, for example in Puccini's *Turandot*.[14]

In response to a journalist's question "why not skate on safer, thicker ice?," Ajne answers:

> Thick ice becomes as interesting as pavement. When too thick it becomes inelastic and **voiceless**, often stricken by cracks, it gets ridges from thermal expansion, and sooner or later snow will entomb the joy of skating. Of course, it is also visually less attractive.[15]

At first, I was captivated by the sound of ice and the singing beyond human comprehension. Then, I found amusement in the skater's comparison of this voice to that of a soprano. Finally, I was moved by Ajne's aversion to thick ice, which is rendered voiceless. The connection between ice, singing, voicelessness, and opera proves puzzling indeed.

The skater serves as a scientific wanderer, meticulously observing atmospheric conditions and the metaphorical "vocal cords of ice." This pursuit of the "frozen voice" encounters many unexpected turns driven by the forces of nature and atmospheric changes. The wanderer's path, involving a blend of scientific considerations, safety precautions, aesthetic choices, and a touch of serendipity, mirrors a durational piece subjected constantly to weather shifts, including temperature, solar activity, winds, and the skater's aesthetic preferences for the timbre of the frozen voice.

In a recent informal conversation following his keynote lecture titled "Symbolic 'Space' as a Time-Function of Sonic Signals" at the conference "Spaces of Musical Production/Production of Musical Spaces," Wolfgang Ernst mentioned myths about frozen sounds in certain cultures.[16] According to these myths, when temperatures plummet during the winter, the air freezes. When a loud acoustic event occurs, the sonic vibrations allegedly freeze too. They are then released when temperatures rise in spring, allowing one to hear the frozen sonic vibration once more. Ernst associated the myth with the mechanism of the phonograph—a machine that engraves sonic vibrations onto the wax, creating a physical line recording of the sound—which highlights our need for the cultural preservation of sounds. I envision that in their frozen state, sounds lose all hierarchical structure, existing simultaneously without order or perspective. At that moment, sounds transform into landscapes.

The same happens with skating, which produces a singing-like sound on elastic black ice. A transformation occurs before the ice becomes too rigid, hence "voiceless." The structure, rhythm, and dynamics of this "frozen singing" flow seamlessly, challenging the singular viewer/listener perspective. The skater's gliding motion generates sounds that emanate in all directions, both within and outside "the view" and the skater's ear. One can never anticipate when or how these sounds will be materialized/projected. This singing, which lacks a singular source, is not directed at any specific path. It occurs as a perpetual singing burst—a vocal eruption devoid of a clear beginning, middle, or end—triggered by the skater's vibrations on the ice. Together, the skater and the ice produce an uncanny vocal yarn.

## Vulnerability: Singing and Drowning

In 2018, Castellucci staged Henze's oratorio, *Das Floß der Medusa* ("The Raft of the Medusa"), as an opera.[17] The narrative draws inspiration from the tragic shipwreck of the French frigate Méduse, dispatched to Senegal in 1816 to re-establish colonial power relations. However, the ship runs aground, prompting the crew to take to lifeboats, leaving behind an improvised raft carrying around one hundred and fifty people. Sadly, only fifteen of them survived after enduring thirteen days of horror. This tragic incident served as the creative impetus for the renowned painting "Le Radeau de la Méduse" (1818–19) by Théodore Géricault.

Castellucci's production is characterized by a massive transparent screen spanning the entire stage. The video was captured at the exact coordinates of the Medusa shipwreck, utilizing a combination of a drone camera, a conventional camera, and underwater filming techniques. The colossal dimension of the screen extending across the entire stage—particularly notable given that the stage at the Dutch National Opera is one of the largest and widest—engulfs viewers completely, engendering an immersive experience for them.

The video displayed on the transparent screen takes the form of a documentary durational piece. A local swimming teacher is filmed floating in the sea for four days until exhaustion. The central focus is on him and the expansive sea surrounding him. The relentless presence of the sea, waves, and wind permeates the footage. Notably, there is no audio—we observe him in silence. This video footage serves as the backdrop for the stage, and various narratives involving singers, choirs, and other characters unfold before it.

As time progresses, it becomes evident that the video also serves as documentation of the harrowing process of drowning. The focus is on the swimmer, or more precisely, the escalating horror he endures as he is slowly engulfed in the agony of drowning. The once robust athlete gradually collapses into exhaustion, each frame revealing the increasing inarticulateness brought on by the horrors of fatigue, cold, breathlessness, and the loss of strength. Castellucci positions every audience member meticulously such that they could comprehend firsthand what it means to fight for one's life in the water—they experience this drowning reality as if it were their own. I could vividly recall the discomfort I felt as the swimmer slowly succumbed to exhaustion. A sense of helplessness pervaded me.

As we witness what appears to be the inevitable drowning of an African man on the immense screen, members of the choir "float" behind a transparent canvas, resembling a school of fish or sea monsters. They sing. Strikingly, we never hear the voice of the drowning man or the sounds of the sea. The horror of drowning is intensified by its silent portrayal on stage. The vulnerability of singing, heightened emotionality, and extreme fragility become even more precarious when confronted with the silent horror of drowning, the work's chief subject matter. The complex interplay of live opera performance and film/video, the political relevance of the Medusa narrative today amidst the ongoing refugee crisis where thousands lose their lives in the Mediterranean, raises the poignant question of who possesses a voice, literally and metaphorically speaking.

The voice of the swimmer, though silent, holds profound significance. It reshapes all the other audible voices on stage, which are ironically overshadowed by the horror of silenced drowning, sinking into it like a black hole.

## Visible: Voice in the Bubble

The final example is Julie Gaultier's short underwater film *Ama*, in which she delivers a personal confession about loss. It is shot in one of the deepest swimming pools on Earth commonly used by apnea divers. Accompanied by post-minimalist repetitive music, *Ama* aligns with the slow-motion movements of the underwater dancer. In the film's opening, it is challenging to recognize that the performance unfolds underwater. It soon becomes evident as the hair motions, clothing fabric, and dancer's movements do not conform to airborne expectations.

The entire choreography, reportedly lasting around 5 minutes, was captured while Gaultier (dancer and choreographer) held a single breath. The most intriguing moment lies at the end of the film, where Gaultier blew out air from her lungs as she rose above the surface. The bubbles of air flew away in slow motion towards the top. Air became visual as we observed a bubble exiting her mouth, invoking the illusion that voice was contained within the bubble. It resembled some kind of silent underwater singing or even screaming. I mused over the possibility that voice was captured in that bubble of air, and once it reached the surface, the bubble would "release" the voice and we would hear it. The film concluded before that moment.

In an attempt to establish a posthuman, post-sonorous conception of voice as "one that acknowledges the provinciality and contingency of its sounded dimension and highlights its many environmental entailments," J. Martin Daughtry describes vocality as a convergence of five processes: gaseous exchange, atmospheric disturbance, sharing of airborne elements between environments (cross-pollution), durational effects as a result of this sharing, and dissolution of boundaries that separate the environments.[18] Daughtry's definition of voice relies on the necessity of breathing and air. However, Gaultier's example of the silent voice that becomes visible directly challenges this perspective.

The "singing ice" that does not breathe, the drowning man who loses his breath, and the dancer who emits a visible but inaudible voice underwater collectively ask us to consider whether voice exists in the absence of breathing. This absence of breath challenges conventional notions of singing and pushes the boundaries of what is traditionally understood as vocal expression. Each of these idiosyncratic situations—the powerful singing ice, the drowning man's voiceless struggle, the underwater dancer's captured vocal—contributes to a broader exploration of the possibilities and limits of vocal expression in the performing arts.

## Notes

1 This work was made with the support of CESEM – Centro de Estudos de Sociologia e Estética Musical—NOVA FCSH, UIDB/00693/20203 and LA/P/0132/2020 with the financial support of FCT, I.P. through National funds.

2 Postopera is opera that is postmodern and postdramatic. A defining feature is the unconventional relationship between the singing voice and the body, as the body–voice construct is being reinvented, making one question conventional audiovisual expectations. Read more about postopera at Jelena Novak, *Postopera: Reinventing the Voice-Body*, London, Routledge, 2015.

3 National Geographic, "Hear the Otherworldly Sounds of Skating on Thin Ice | National Geographic," 2018, https://www.youtube.com/watch?app=desktop&v=v3O9vNi-dkA.

4 Dutch National Opera & Ballet, "Das Floß Der Medusa by Hans Werner Henze," YouTube, 2018, https://www.youtube.com/watch?v=zflExizdesE.

5 The film is available at Julie Gautier, "AMA - a Short Film by Julie Gautier," YouTube, 2018, https://www.youtube.com/watch?app=desktop&v=bdBuDg7mrT8.

6 Humming, whistling, artless singing (like singing under the shower) in films falls in the cracks of film studies. It is taken for granted as it does not belong to the film's soundtrack. But it still produces the meanings discussed in Claudia Gorbman, "Artless Singing," *Music, Sound and the Moving Image* 5, no. 2 (2011): 157–71.
7 Ana Vujanovic, "Zusammen mäandern. Neue Tendenzen in der Landschaftsdramaturgie ('Meandering Together: New Problems in Landscape Dramaturgy')," in *Postdramaturgien*, ed. Jan Deck et al., trans. Ana Vujanovic (Germany: Neofelis, 2020), https://www.academia.edu/34879796/Meandering_together_New_problems_in_landscape_dramaturgy_2017_.; Ana Vujanovic, "Landscape Dramaturgy: 'Space after Perspective,'" in *Thinking Alongside*, ed. Ingri Midgard Fiksdal (Oslo: 07 Media, 2018), 159–70.
8 Wolfgang Ernst, *Sonic Time Machines: Explicit Sound, Sirenic Voices, and Implicit Sonicity* (Amsterdam: Amsterdam University Press, 2016).
9 J. Martin Daughtry, "Call and Response (Or the Lack Thereof): Atmospheric Voices and Distributed Selves," *Sensate*, 2021, https://sensatejournal.com/call-and-response-or-the-lack-thereof-atmospheric-voices-and-distributed-selves/.
10 Vujanovic, "Landscape Dramaturgy: 'Space after Perspective,'" 164.
11 Ibid.
12 Royce Vavrek's program note, "In Opera, the Close-up is the Aria" for the opera *Melancholia*, was first published in Swedish as "Filmens närbild finns i arian" in the program book of the opera in the Royal Swedish Opera in 2023.
13 National Geographic, "Hear the Otherworldly Sounds of Skating on Thin Ice | National Geographic."
14 Amy Rankin, "How Skating on Thin Ice Creates Laser-Like Sounds," *National Geographic*, January 30, 2018, https://www.nationalgeographic.com/adventure/article/skating-thin-black-ice-creates-sound-nordic-spd.
15 Ibid.
16 International conference "Spaces of Musical Production / Production of Musical Spaces" organized by *Sound, Stage, Screen* took place from 3-5 November 2023 at Triennale, Milano.
17 Henze wrote it as a Requiem for Che Guevara, and set it to a text by Ernst Schnabel. The work is considered to reflect the composer's open alignment with left wing politics.
18 Daughtry, "Call and Response (Or the Lack Thereof): Atmospheric Voices and Distributed Selves."

# 8 Pastoral Paradox

## Staging Ted Hearne's *Farming* (2023) and Kate Soper's *The Hunt* (2023)

*Ashley Kelly Tata*

The singers gaze at the sky. The sound "ahhhhh" naturally decaying in the air. A hawk floats, circling without a flap, seemingly held aloft by the exhale of twenty-four choral voices. A fermata. The wind breathes, rustles hair, fabric, and late-summer tall grasses. Somewhere, a microphone artificially amplifies this natural accident. Heads drift. Framing the singers is a proscenium of crystal blue sky with wisps of cloud, a deck of tilled, dark brown farmland, and the hard legs of a dark green tree line. A wormhole exhales open, and the imagination travels to this land before William Penn. Before the colonizers' boot. Before the "ahhhhh" of Pennsylvania.

The beat drops. The wormhole bubble pops. The Cagean improvisation record scratches, and the singers march into formation as they sing, "Cuh - Cuh - Cuh - Cuh - Country. Country. Country. Country. My God has given it to me. Country. My Country was confirmed to me."

These words are quoted from William Penn's 1681 "Letter to Robert Turner," in which the Quaker colonialist described the land given to him by King Charles II of England. Land the King would never see or set foot on. A land that was now serving as the scenic design of Ted Hearne's *Farming*, performed by the choral group The Crossing in a premiere directed by myself in the summer of 2023.

The land as a scenic design was a critical part of the commission for this premiere. In that season, many works commissioned by The Crossing foregrounded the land. The picture that was painted to me by the commissioners of *Farming* was a desire to create pieces that would not be an intervention on the land, rather an extension of it. The hope was that the performance would accentuate the site on which it was being performed: a piece of farmland in Bucks County, Pennsylvania. Spending a summer making a new opera in this pastoral setting sounded idyllic.

This approach to creating a work could be labeled as "site-specific" or "environmental." In either or both cases, it is not a unique or innovative ask. This year marks the fiftieth anniversary of the publication of Richard Schechner's *Environmental Theater.* There is nothing *avant garde* about staging something outdoors. In my own career, site-specific staging is often driven by pragmatic reasons. Over fifteen years ago, when I was exclusively self-producing, a $25

DOI: 10.4324/9781003462286-12

Parks Permit from New York City was my only viable path to securing a performance venue. What has evolved over time, which makes some of these efforts seem new or different today than they did perhaps fifteen or fifty years ago, is the positioning of the natural environment in relation to the works themselves. In the Parks' system, the environment may have been *al fresco* but was far from being "natural." There were monuments, amphitheaters, and sculpture parks all designed by humans, which I would frame as sites of performance.

The initial goal of the setting for *Farming* would be its lack of human construction. Human voices and an open field would be the elements used to compose a *mise en scène*. This seeming void presented the kind of terror and thrill of staring at a blank canvas. The human bodies of the chorus would become the architecture that defines a perspective. The goal of working in such a way mirrors practices in the fields of visual arts, design, and architecture that, in the Anthropocene era, look forward to a post-human future. Like the work of Neri Oxman, whose Silk Pavilion series engages in a "collaboration" between robots and silk worms that coax worms to spin sheets of silk, and Natalie Jerimenjenko's TreeXOffice in which a tree is the landlord of an office space, the rental of which pays for the upkeep of local parks, these works are less about representing nature than creating a synergy between humans and nature.[1]

Ted Hearne is a composer whose work is associated with the amplified, sampled, auto-tuned, and glitch-laden. His *Law of Mosaics* (2013) includes "Palindrome for Andrew Norman," a work "constructed entirely of samples lifted from other pieces of music."[2] *The Source* (2014) uses interactive autotune on movements such as "Smoke When Bird Nears," which also includes samples from the soundtrack to Hitchcock's *The Birds* and a "classic American rendition of the song *Smoke gets in your eyes*."[3] Hearne might not be the first composer one would think of to write a choral piece about the land that would respect its more-or-less natural state. Commissioning Hearne for this project created an inherent tension that would continuously provide the artistic resource of destabilization.

As with earlier works such as *Katrina Ballads* as well as *The Source* and *Songs from the Bench*, *Farming* reflects a continuation of a project in which Hearne draws on primary source documents from US history as the text of a libretto. The farmland where the premiere took place in Pennsylvania is not far from where William Penn and Tamanend of the Lenape signed the treaty of Shackamaxon—a treaty later used by Penn's sons to cheat the Lenape of their land. Hearne mined source material from letters written by William Penn to and about the Lenape people, as well as various public addresses made by Jeff Bezos. Hearne accounts for the juxtaposition of these sources in the following quote:

> Although they were born more than three centuries apart, when their words were laid next to each other as if in a conversation, Penn and Bezos started to sound to me like they possessed a similar worldview: one that frames your own intentions as benevolent, your own mission as destined by God, and thus your own actions (as exploitative or violent as they may be) as a boon to humanity.[4]

*Figure 8.1* Rehearsal at Kings Oaks Farm. Lighting by Pablo Santiago, Carolina Ortiz and The Sun.

Kings Oaks Farm, the current name of the farm where the premiere of *Farming* was staged, as shown in Figure 8.1 above, is transitioning into an organic farm. Turning our chemically saturated farmlands into those that grow "organic" produce takes labor, attention, and time. Fortunately, there is a timeframe for this detoxifying process: three years.[5] Staged nature can represent the psychological state of characters (Shakespeare's King Lear and the Heath), the zeitgeist of a society (the mysterious sound coming from somewhere in the Orchard of Chekhov's *A Cherry Orchard*), and in some rare cases, even anthropomorphized as characters (Audrey in *Little Shop of Horrors*). In *Anatomy of Criticism*, Northrop Frye writes that,

> The mode of romantic comedy corresponding to the elegiac is best described as idyllic, and its chief vehicle is the pastoral. [...] the idyllic cannot equal the introversion of the elegiac, but it preserves the theme of escape from society to the extent of idealizing a simplified life in the country or on the frontier [...] The close association with animal and vegetable nature [...] recurs in the sheep and pleasant pastures (or the cattle and ranches) of the idyllic, [...] such imagery is often used, as it is in the Bible, for the theme of salvation.[6]

What's striking is how persistently the "idyllic" can adhere to any reading of a work that takes place in nature. I became aware that I was carrying this presumption with me until we were on land. Until I really listened to the demos of Hearne's compositions. Until we really started to have a conversation about the falsity of claiming that this farmland could represent an idyllic "escape from society" or "salvation" as Northrop Frye suggests the pastoral would have us do. In the same way that this work invited a critical view of the Quaker colonizer represented by the figure of William Penn, the desire to make a work devoid of human intervention would perpetuate a lie of the land that felt like reinforcing tropes, which felt offensive to the nature of our project. Asking the land to lie about itself seemed like a violation. She is trying to detox. So the design went in another direction: we considered what it means to be at a time when humans and corporations are paradoxically trying to bring the natural back into our manufactured environments. There are office plans that incorporate plastic plants to win and influence people: "daylight" spectra lightbulbs in fun houses like Las Vegas casinos or 24-hour Apple Stores that keep shoppers in a perpetual consumer standard time. The consequence of this kind of hubris has been portrayed in theater as a warning to humanity since the time of the ancient Greeks when Aeschylus portrayed the tragedy resulting from the hubris of Xerxes bridging the Hellespont in *The Persians*.

The inverse seemed to be the less hubristic choice in our case. We relaxed our initial concept of not intervening on the land. The lighting designers, Pablo Santiago and Carolina Ortiz, created a lighting design that incorporated the natural light of the sun bounced off of reflectors and moved into dusk, where industrial Beebe lamps would take over. These lamps, used in contemporary agricultural practices, allow workers to farm well past the days' end. This way, the light sources could effectively cross-fade from nature to human control. We added elements that filter humans from nature. We placed a refrigerator on the land. Leafy greens became a currency with which to bribe consumers. Nia Easley's work on the design team incorporated her practice as a visual artist, whose work interrogates place and history and engages with the community. She created a series of thirty municipal-looking signs that provoked a discourse around the origin and history of the word "farming," including "To hire out the labor of (cattle, people, etc.)." One of these signs is shown in Figure 8.2. Easley also farmed out some of the labor of making artwork for the piece, utilizing an AI image generator to create depictions of Jeff Bezos and William Penn embracing in Amazon warehouses.

Ultimately, our hubris (like Xerxes's) came back on us. Climate change in the northeastern United States has resulted in some unpredictable rainy seasons. Flood-like waters inundated our opening weekend. The whole production had to move into a sheltered space, fundamentally changing the design. This unanticipated forced re-setting manifested the history of a land staked out in deceit, blood, and the viewing of the earth we walk on as a resource to be exchanged for money. Of seeing human beings as a resource. The performers were confined into a warehouse-like structure, evoking the working conditions of the online click-to-buy era. The only skyline the audience could see was reflected in the aviator

*Figure 8.2* A sign designed by Nia Easley for Ted Hearne's Farming.

glasses worn by a character who sings an Uber Eats Twitter feed posting: "Why yes, we're open. What are/Ordering? Why yes, we're open. What are you."[7]

We are what we order.

## Kate Soper's *The Hunt* (2023)

It's October 2023. A singer stands in a stark white light surrounded by darkness as she sings:

> I have had enough —
> border-pinks, clove-pinks, wax-lilies, herbs, sweet-cress.
> O for some sharp swish of a branch — there is no scent of resin in this place,
> no taste of bark, of course weeds, aromatic, astringent —
> This beauty

…without strength, chokes out life.
I want to break,
scatter these pink stalks, snap off their spiced heads,
…
spread the path with twigs,
…
trail great pine branches, hurled from some far-off wood right across the
melon-patch, break pear and quince— leave half-trees, torn, twisted
but showing the fight was valiant. Oh…to blot out this garden
…to find a new beauty in some terrible
wind tortured place.[8]

As the lights return to normal, the tall plywood wall is illuminated behind her. This wall built of the taming of trees casts an ascetic and cool pall on the actions taken by the trio of sopranos at the heart of Kate Soper's *The Hunt*, which premiered in a staging directed by myself at the Miller Theater. It is a story about female-presenting and non-binary virgins who are hired by a king to lure the unicorn into a clearing so the unicorn can be captured, killed, and their horns harvested for the power they bestow on their owner.

This was the second work of 2023 that I staged, which involved the element of nature as a force to be reckoned with or reconciled with. We went from farmland to the shadow of plywood. Plywood is a regular feature in theatrical design. The appropriation of the minimal aesthetic in art and architecture from the works of artists like Donald Judd and Richard Serra tends to bring a cool sophistication and edginess to the stage. "This," the material seems to announce, "is the presentation of a work by someone who is in control of their form." To harness a natural and ancient superorganism like a tree and cut it down into 1/4″ thick, four feet by eight feet sheets of cross-hatched plywood stuck together by a chemically or animal-based adherent to reinforce and limit the risk of warping is a testament to the machine and consumerist ages for which it has been mass-produced and mass-utilized. Plywood is utilitarian and can bring warmth and "natural" wood grain to the spaces it graces. "Plywood still looked like wood. After all, the plies were very thin sheets unrolled from a smooth, stout Douglas fir bole by a gigantic lathe. A plywood panel's face showed the grain of the tree. But the wedding of synthetic resins and plant fiber initiated even more plastic-wood combinations, until the chemical overwhelmed the organic."[9] The prevalence and false promise in its use give it an insidious feel, like the attempt to bring a "natural" feel to a production staged on colonized farmland.

The scenic designer, Aoshuang Zhang, endeavored to create a landscape that changed with the evolving agency of the characters. Over the course of the opera, the trio find their own power and end up making the difficult choice to stay where they are in order to simultaneously prevent the same fate from befalling any other virgin and save the life of the unicorn. Soper and I workshopped the final scene multiple times to strike the right tone. An image of the final scene is shown in Figure 8.3 below. At some point, it became clear that the characters were able to gain agency by availing themselves of the natural resources of the clearing. Zhang's environment functioned to emphasize this. At the beginning of the opera, we witness the characters being served processed and prepackaged food (bologna sandwiches) by a surveillance system-triggered, autonomous dumb-waiter. By the end of the opera, the characters are involved in creating a seed library to produce their own food, medicines, and potions as necessary.

Recently, I have been resistant to minimalist stage designs. This comes from a sense of urgency to create audacious, baroque, overzealous, and amorous works that embrace the theatrical form and embodied performance. To jumpstart our senses and aesthetic reception after years of pandemic. Additionally, I have always loved the audacity of the operatic form. But there are many factors involved in a design. As is the case with many contemporary operas I have directed, the singers in this work were not only singing intricate and delicate compositions; they were also self-accompanied on violin and ukulele. I wanted to make sure that the characters' arcs were amplified in the arc of design. The design dramaturgy would have to evoke the physical locations inhabited by the characters and allow that space to change as their

*Figure 8.3* Last scene of Kate Soper's *The Hunt*.

Photo by Rob Davidson for Miller Theatre at Columbia University. Pictured from left to right: Christiana Cole, Brett Umlauf, and Hirona Amamiya. Scenic design, Aoshuang Zhang. Costume Design, Terese Wadden. Lighting Design, Masha Tsimmring. Video Design, Camilla Tassi. Hair and Make-up Design, Anika Seitu.

relationships with their own bodies and the world shift. As in any production, my aim is to bring together all the elements to overtly and subconsciously convey a message so that an audience member who is sitting in the theater might use their whole body as a sense organ that perceives the event unfolding in time and space. A scenic design is not a static set piece. In this pastoral mode, the characters would liberate nature through their self-liberation.

Throughout the piece, one of the characters, Rue (who is also the group's resident gardener, herbalist, and closeted witch), talks of sensing that there will be rain. Similar to a post-apocalyptic, colonized landscape that stakes Didi and Gogo to their places in Beckett's *Waiting for Godot*, Rue's consistent bringing up of the promise of rain only to be reminded that "it never, ever, ever rains" starts to fill in a landscape that is undergoing a certain kind of ecological devastation. The reasons for this are never made clear. A major turning point of the narrative is when (spoiler) the sky opens up and it downpours. The sky must have been holding it in for ages because it proceeds to rain for weeks. When the virgins finally return to their clearing, the environment is overgrown and lush. This coincides with their sexual awakenings. The characters of Fleur and Briar reveal their mutual attraction, and Rue finally gins up the courage to seduce the Stable Boy. The flowering of nature's arrival brought on by the rainstorm encourages the characters to take bella donna, a natural herb, which elicits psychotropic responses. It is in the throes of this trip that the Virgins finally see the Unicorn. Whether it is the drugs that bring this about, the rain, or sexual anticipation is not entirely clear. I'd like to think that, like a mycelial network, these are all linked, and none of them can happen without the other.

And what about the plywood? In an elegantly engineered design, Zhang created a pivot at the center of each of three very large panels of plywood. As the virgins re-enter the clearing, they turn the panels to reveal thick patches of ivy on what was the upstage side of the wall. As we move into the final section of the work, a further transition occurs. Once the virgins have consummated their passion for their respective objects of affection and are no longer virginal, the three characters leave the large panels ajar, revealing strands of pink ivy in the land beyond the wall. One gets the sense that the giant plywood wall had scarcely been able to keep out the wild pink ivy creeping just beyond its perimeter. The singers rally with a parodic punk version of a song we had heard at the beginning of the opera. Presumably, it was a work that had been written by the King, or his court composer (Soper?) to be performed as an audition song in order to book the gig that we've just witnessed with the Virgins, basically, quiet quit.[10] This tune now becomes a kind of protest anthem in the vein of a Pussy Riot performance. "The unicorn can't be taken alive! The unicorn can't be taken alive! THE UNICORN CAN'T BE TAKEN ALIVE!"

All the while, the male-presenting staff of groundskeepers are slowly sweeping the grounds where the pink ivy dangles. The regular and persistent attempt to, if not outright control, the nature that surrounds us reminds us of our inability to relent the control we must exert over at least the curation of the natural world. The writing of ancient works of theater in the past was a way to try to appease and control the unnatural forces that threaten to destroy human beings. Today, we can try to give agency back to nature in our performances, but it may take a long time to find that idyllic way to work in true synthesis with the natural world. What these experiments in synthesis have left me contemplating is the difficulty of de-centering the human in representative forms like theater or opera. But I intend to continue on the task of a virtual reality opera about trees, *VirtualRealiTree*—a logical impossibility.

## Notes

1 Neri Oxman, "Mission," accessed December 7, 2023, https://oxman.com/mission.
2 Ted Hearne, "LAW OF MOSAICS (2013, 30 MIN.)," 2013, https://www.tedhearne.com/works/law-of-mosaics.
3 Ted Hearne, "THE SOURCE," accessed December 30, 2023, https://www.tedhearne.com/project-details/2015/10/9/the-source.
4 Ted Hearne, "Farming Chronicles" newsletter, emailed to email list, August, 8, 2023.
5 Peter Coy, "Making Farms Organic Is Paying Off," *The New York Times*, January 27, 2023, sec. Opinion, https://www.nytimes.com/2023/01/27/opinion/investing-profitable-organic-farming.html.
6 Northrop Frye, *Anatomy of Criticism: Four Essays* (Princeton: Princeton University Press, 1957), 43.
7 Ted Hearne, *UberEats; Farming,* June 2023.
8 Kate Soper, abr. H. D. from "Sheltered Garden," *The Hunt*, October, 2023.
9 Janet Ore, "Mobile Home Syndrome: Engineered Woods and the Making of a New Domestic Ecology in the Post—World War II Era," *Technology and Culture* 52, no. 2 (2011): 271.
10 Cal Newport, "The Year in Quiet Quitting," *The New Yorker*, December 29, 2022, https://www.newyorker.com/culture/2022-in-review/the-year-in-quiet-quitting.

# 9 Interview with Pamela Z

*Pamela Z and Jingyi Zhang*

*JZ:* I had the chance to experience both your operas *Wunderkabinet* (2006) and *Times*$^3$ (2021). I'm struck by how fresh they sound, and their genre-defying qualities. Can you share with us more about how your intermedia artistic persona, vocal background, and technical wizardry shape your overall approach to opera conception, composition, and performance?

*PZ:* Well, I think it's interesting because I've always had a hard time settling into any genre. *Wunderkabinet* is definitely an opera, but I have many other multimedia performance works that could also fall into that category. *Times*$^3$ was indeed commissioned by a company that normally presents and produces operas. But it's really a fixed media sound work. But perhaps it could be viewed as an opera in a way. I don't know. It's interesting because, if it's an opera, it would be the first opera I know of that has no live performance on stage, no movement, no blocking, no individual characters, or libretto. Rather, it has a sonic landscape that explores something. And sampled speaking voices, which I use a lot in my work for both for their sonic qualities and content. But I find it an honor and, at once, amusing that the piece is being viewed as an opera.

*Times*$^3$ is very site-specific, bizarrely, because it was created pretty early in the lockdown or right in the midst of it. Originally, when they asked me to make that piece, I thought I would go there, but I was locked down in San Francisco in my studio doing a lot of commissioned work, live streaming concerts from the studio, and so forth. But what I couldn't do, at that time, was get on a plane and go to New York and walk around in Times Square. So it was all done remotely, even though I do think it's about a very specific site. And originally, the intent was that people would download that sound file and listen to it while they were physically in Times Square. But after I finished the piece, I felt pretty strongly that it's almost better to listen to it in the comfort of your home on a really good pair of headphones with your eyes closed. And just imagine yourself in

DOI: 10.4324/9781003462286-13

Times Square. And now, with Time Squares back to being crazy and busy, if you went there and tried listening to the piece, I don't think you'd even hear half of it because that's too loud there.

*JZ:* I was deeply fascinated by *Times³*, especially how you're not only directly drawing on these interviews with people from different backgrounds who are familiar with Times Square, but the multifaceted ways you're utilizing the voice as a medium of composition—*logos* (focusing on words and what they say) and the *echos* (how words sound, their musical properties). Can you talk a little more about your creative process, your interest in found sounds/speech, and how, in this piece, you've managed to draw out something so poetic and musical from these materials?

*PZ:* For a very long time now, I've been deeply involved with making music from speech sounds. Sometimes they are samples of my own voice but, quite frequently, I get speech sounds from interviewing people. And if possible, I get them to come to my studio and I put them in my isolation booth where I can get very pristine, clean recordings, and be able to isolate fragments of their speech – sometimes full sentences, but mostly just small phrases, words, syllables, or even phonemes. And when you start chopping language down to those elements, if the recording isn't very, very clean, then it begins to not read anymore. In order for it to read as actual words, syllables, or speech sounds, the recording needs to be clean without any background noise. And so, the best-case scenario is I start with really well-recorded samples, but sometimes I don't have that luxury.

For example, when I made *Times³*, all those interviews had to be done on Zoom. We sent people a microphone and an audio interface and trained them over zoom how to set it up so they could get excellent quality recording. And they varied greatly. Then, I cut them up and built little phrases or little fragments of speech, and made a library of named clips so I could actually search for them. Then, I began working with collaging them in tracks of ProTools. I started pulling out my favorite little fragments, listened to them, and tried to discern the actual pitches and rhythms embedded in that speech. Next, I transcribed them and played them into MIDI. Sometimes, I learnt to sing them myself or moved them into a notation software like Sibelius where I created parts for string players or other instrumentalists to play. I hired a violinist, a trumpet player, a cellist, and transcribed parts for them. Next, I sent them the scores as PDFs and directed them over Zoom to play those parts and record them as well as they could. Then, they sent them back to me and I laid them down into the piece. But a lot of those things that I wrote for them were mimicking precise speech sounds from some of the language in the interviews. I've been writing a lot of chamber music where all of the string parts are coming from fragments of speech that I've sampled.

*JZ:* I really enjoyed watching *Wunderkabinet*! There's this enchanting, fantastic element which makes it really operatic in a way by capturing opera's too-muchness. Can you tell us more about what drives you and Matthew Brubeck to collaborate on this opera, and how the collaboration process went?

*PZ:* What inspired us to make *Wunderkabinet* is The Museum of Jurassic Technology in Los Angeles. Every time I'm there, I always try to visit that museum. It's this very odd cabinet of curiosities and it sort of masquerades as just a museum, but in fact, it's the brainchild and conceptual artwork of an artist named David Wilson. He won a MacArthur and he used his MacArthur money to make that museum. And it's echoing all those Wunderkammer-type of places where you walk in and see dark oak, glass-topped vitrines, with things underneath that you're supposed to look at. And they're always pseudo-scientific or historic, but they're all very odd and you're always wondering if it's real or invented. That museum was such an inspiration to both Matthew and me!

Matthew had the idea based on this area called Letters to the Observatory, which foregrounded mental illness. There were people writing rather strange letters, and one particular person was Alice May Williams, who is my character in *Wunderkabinet*. She's writing these very long, heartfelt letters to warn people at the observatory to be careful because she thinks they're going to hurt the alien creatures that live on the moon. We were both touched by those letters and wanted to make this into an opera.

*Wunderkabinet* was my first ever co-composed project. And we did it in segments, like much of my other works. There were parts that Matthew mainly composed and others that I mainly composed. Usually, we would then add layers to each other's sections, so it was really very collaboratively made. And we worked with a video artist, Christina McPhee, who built the multichannel video for each section.

*JZ:* Did you first have the visual conception and text before you wrote the music?

*PZ:* I think what came first was shooting all that video at the museum and capturing the text from the exhibitions. I used a lot of those texts as libretto. It's very rare that I write music set to somebody else's texts but, in this case, the lion's share of the libretto comes from placards at David Wilson's museum or actual text heard in the earphones when you listen at the museum. I used some of it exactly as it was, but I twisted most of it and adjusted a little. And I invented some things too. But each little scene was inspired by one of the exhibits in that museum. Then, I built a narrative around that to pull it all together and came up with this idea that my character actually didn't hear back from the people at the observatory. So she decided that she needed to get on a boat, come to the United States, find them, and talk to them. And so, she was trying to go to the observatory but instead ended up at Wunderkabinet, which is The Museum of Jurassic Technology.

*JZ:* Both of you were not only creators but performers of the opera, and in your case, you're also a director! I'm struck by your hyphenated status in the conception and performance of *Wunderkabinet*, and could you tell us how you managed to navigate among these very different artistic roles?

*PZ:* I've always worked in an isolated way on my large-scale performance works. I wrote all the music for them, decided on the order, the blocking etc. And I would hire a lighting designer to work on the lighting, sometimes a visual person to build the video part. But even with them, I would give them a lot of direction about what I wanted.

But something I've always found challenging, even though I always felt I should, was to hire a director. I just couldn't manage to do that. And it's partially because I was always slammed right up against deadlines to finish, so it was hard to have something polished enough for a director to actually work on with me. Instead, I would just work on it myself, or ask a favor from a friend who's a good movement artist and have them come in towards the end and give me some pointers about movement. But mostly, I worked on my own, not to say that I'm the best person for that. It was just very challenging for me to work another person into the schedule of getting the piece made. I do think that a lot of dramaturgical elements were molded by the music, and sometimes those ideas are already in my head before I begin working on the music, and I know that I want to make something around them. It just varies from section to section and from piece to piece.

*JZ:* You played this dyslexic opera singer Alemap Zed and made her sing her arias in reverse. When the narrator remarked on how, despite her disorder, her voice was considered so beautiful that she continued performing arias that audiences loved, I was particularly struck by this character who seems to be making a meta-statement on opera and opera singing itself. Opera is often sung in foreign languages, but even if it's sung in English, it's still incomprehensible to us. But we're nonetheless transfixed. In the case of Alemap Z who sings in reverse, it doesn't make her sing any *less* beautiful. Can you perhaps talk a bit about what prompted you to come up with this dyslexic character, the idea of singing in reverse, and your experience of embodying this character on stage?

*PZ:* In The Museum of Jurassic Technology, one of the exhibits is about an opera singer who has a little backstory. She doesn't sing backwards, but it was one of those places where I thought it would be fun to create my own version of this character, and create my own aria for her. And I can't remember what got me started on the reverse thing, but I do know that I went through a period where I was really having fun with time-compressing and time-expanding sounds. I also had done a lot at some point with reversing, and really prided myself in the fact that I could learn to say things backwards and then reversing them so that they would sound forwards, but like almost in a Martian accent. And it's funny, I did that before I ever saw David Lynch's *Twin Peaks*. There were dream sequences in *Twin Peaks* which were filmed by having the actors learn their lines backwards. And it was all played reversed. So, they had to walk backwards, gesture backwards, sit down when they were supposed to stand up, and then deliver their lines, which they had memorized backwards. And many saw those dream sequences and didn't really know what was happening. They just knew they looked and sounded strange. But the minute I heard them, I recognized what it was because I had been doing that for years, learning to say things backwards, recording myself and then playing them in reverse. You can't just reverse the spelling; you have to reverse every syllable, every sound that's in that word. I would record myself and then play it backwards which just sounds strange because the attacks are weird. But what was interesting is that I used to just do it with audio. I never did it with video. And then I saw that David Lynch did it and I thought it was great. That's probably what made me realize I could do the Alemap aria, and that it could be video with her singing backwards. But, to make it, I sang it forwards and recorded the video and then the video was reversed. For a later performance, I did actually learn the backwards version of the aria, and sang that way live. It wasn't a full opera but a small performance, but I really love that. I actually want to do more of that.

*JZ:* All your works have shown this fascination with the human voice, electronics, and other creative intermedia possibilities, which interestingly predates a lot of what's happening in the contemporary and experimental opera scene today. There's also this emerging phenomenon of collaborating with non-traditional artists like sound artists, improvisor, multimedia artist who inject new energy and possibilities into opera as a genre. What are your thoughts on these interdisciplinary collaborations, and in what ways do you think it contributes to the future of opera?

*PZ:* I feel that the interdisciplinary nature of a lot of the work that we have today really reflects opera from the very earliest times. Opera has always been interdisciplinary. There's always something visual, there's singing, there's a language written by someone, there's movement, there's a lot of theatricality, and there's often ballet inserted into scenes. So, opera has a history of being interdisciplinary, and that's not really new. But when we enter the computer era, "multimedia" took on a host of other meanings—people began to assume that it had something to do with computers when it actually means what the word actually means—multimedia, different mediums. But "multimedia" came to refer to situations where computers were involved, which was ironic because computer is just one medium. I do think that there's a very long history of opera being interdisciplinary, but because of the new technology that we have, and its telecommunication aspect, there are more possibilities now. So that's interesting and irreversible.

When it comes to performance formats, I noticed now that a lot of venues are presenting in person again, and they're also all offering a streaming possibility. Audiences can either attend the performance in-person or they can get a link and watch the streaming, which is a very good documentation of the event unfolding in real time. But the other major innovation is that people can participate together in performances and broadcast them in real time.

Before the pandemic, I used to do this series of chamber performances called the ROOM Series. And it used to take place in this little performance gallery on the first floor of the building that I live in. And when I came back from Rome in March 2020, I wanted to do a ROOM Series concert, but the room that I previously used was no longer available. And I couldn't have a live performance with a PA with the audience in the room. So, I did a streaming version of the ROOM Series, and I had a concert, and that was the first concert where I had one artist in Oakland, one artist in San Francisco (me), and one artist in Verona, Italy, and we all performed solo. And we all performed together at the end of the concert.

And it's not the first time I've done something like that. Actually, before the pandemic and before anybody had ever heard of Zoom, I had a ROOM Series concert where I wanted double-reed players. I had chosen three of them, and then after having booked the performance and waiting for the performance to begin, one of the double reed players got a post at Oberlin. And I said, let's do it over Skype. We didn't have Zoom yet. And we had her on Skype, and we had a big projection up on the upstage wall of the stage, and Dana Jessen was on there playing her bassoon, and then the rest of us were in the room and we each played solo. And then we did a quartet with Dana Jessen, Sarah Schoenbeck, and Kyle Bruckmann, oboe, and two bassoons. And then, I played with voice electronics. I still have documentation of that show. And I'm proud that we made that show. But now, it's become so commonplace to have people do remote performances together, with the invention of new software to remove latency issues. So this is something that comes from the COVID era, which is here to stay. So, that's probably one thing that will contribute to the future of opera.

# Part IV

# Creative Possibilities of Transmedia Dramaturgy

# 10 Transmedia, Tradition, and Music in Contemporary Japanese Performing Arts

*Krisztina Rosner*

Transmedia describes a "structured relationship between different media platforms and practices."[1] Distinct from multimedia or cross-platform, transmedia approaches are multimodal, intertextual, and dispersed. According to Henry Jenkins, experiences are distributed across platforms "so that the audience must actively work, often through networked consumption, to assemble the pieces."[2] As Robert Pratten states, transmedia storytelling as "a design philosophy" and "umbrella term" refers to a project and production development that aspires to "create synergy between the content and a focus on an emotional, participatory experience for the audience."[3] It operates on the assumption that "the whole is more satisfying than the sum of the parts" and there is an "euphoria of collecting the pieces."[4] In this chapter, I aim to illuminate an emerging phenomenon in the Japanese performance arts, which reconsiders and reframes tradition, opera, and music theater through the integration of contemporary transmedia aesthetics.

The one-night-only performance of *Star Wars Kabuki – Three Shining Swords*, featuring kabuki star Ichikawa Ebizō XI[5] as lead actor, is a kabuki rendition of the epic American space opera saga that premiered in Tokyo in 2019, which sets the stage for my extended inquiry into recent transmedia projects in Japan. The second case study examines what we could call Vocaloid operas, featuring Vocaloid star Hatsune Miku performing Tomita Isao's *Symphony Ihatov* (2012) and Shibuya Keiichiro's *The End* (2012). The appearance of a Vocaloid character in the genre of opera and music theater provokes further reflections on techno-animism and posthumanism. Besides focusing on traditional performances like *Chō-kabuki* that combine cutting-edge technology, I investigate other media platforms that draw on transmediality, such as the smartphone application *INTO* developed by the leading kabuki and film management company Shochiku. Then, I analyze *Madama Butterfly*, directed by Ichihara Satoko in 2021, at the Theater Neumarkt in Zurich. This new production, which radically subverts Giocamo Puccini's original, questions stereotypical representations of otherness and gender. Finally, I turn to Okada Toshiki's *Metamorphosis of a Living Room* to rethink the relationship between music and theater. Commissioned by

DOI: 10.4324/9781003462286-15

the Wiener Festwochen and premiered at the Klangforum Vienna in 2023, this performance reflects a collaboration between theater director Okada Toshiki and composer Fujikura Dai. A serious examination of these transmedia projects provides a valuable opportunity for us to pay attention to the seismic shifts in technology brought about by the pandemic, which asks us to rethink notions such as (tele-) presence, flatness, and the nonhuman condition.

In this instance of "media franchise meet[ing] media franchise" or the transmedia "fusion of worlds," *Star Wars Kabuki – Three Shining Swords* was performed in Tokyo, featuring one of the most popular kabuki stars, Ichikawa Ebizō XI, and his six-year-old son, Shinnosuke. The preparation for the show had been kept secret, but the brief thirty-minute performance took place one night only in November 2019, just a few days before the premiere of the latest installation of Star Wars, *The Rise of Skywalker*, thus attracting intense media attention.

Preceded by an introduction of the androids, inviting remarks like "aren't they cute?" the show opened with the famous theme song, which pervaded the kabuki stage. Instead of regurgitating the well-known story, the plot focuses on three short episodes. Lightsabers are replaced by Japanese swords, and the names of the characters adopt their Japanese characters: Kylo Ren is switched to Kairennosuke (魁連之助), Luke to Ruku (琉空), Leia to Reian (澪殷), Han Solo to Hanzo (半蔵), and Jedi to Judai (壽臺). Ebizō himself plays three characters. The audiovisual effects demonstrate the fusion of various traditions and performance genres. Several musical themes are played on the shamisen and drums, and the stage set merges animation with kabuki, particularly the quick and glamorous costume changes that are characteristic of the genre.

The star of the performance was Ebizō, who has become one of the most renowned figures not only in kabuki but also in the broader entertainment industry in Japan. In his mid-forties, the heir of the renowned Ichikawa kabuki family was to change his stage name from Ichikawa Ebizō XI to the prestigious name of his Ichikawa Danjūrō XIII, symbolizing the promotion within the traditional kabuki family line. The much-awaited succession ceremony was expected to take place in 2020, but it had to be rescheduled due to the pandemic. The ceremony was eventually held in 2023, and Japanese fashion giant Uniqlo designed a kabuki-themed T-shirt collection in commemoration of this epic succession event. As the official Uniqlo promotion material states,

> Art and resolve are passed down over generations in kabuki, the traditional Japanese performing art that emerged during the early seventeenth-century. Even today, more than four hundred years later, the art form continues to inspire and fascinate. […] Danjūrō himself explains how the T-shirts in this collection reflect the traditions and future of kabuki.[6]

Kabuki has a long history of inspiring popular culture. This recent project of transforming the aesthetics represented by glamourous kabuki costumes into mass-market T-shirts merges three major players of the entertainment and fashion industry: Ichikawa Danjūrō, Shochiku, and Uniqlo. As a result of their collaboration, marketable merchandise and collectible memorabilia are created and dispersed, thus contributing to the grand transmedia puzzle.

Another major foray into transmedia performance is reflected in the development of the smartphone application *INTO*, also spearheaded by the giant kabuki and entertainment management company Shochiku. The application uses Augmented Reality (AR) "to bring kabuki performances to life wherever you may be, at any given time."[7] AR and the volumetric 360° video technology transform the audiences' surroundings into a stage on which the kabuki actor Kataoka Ainosuke delivers a six-minute performance. *INTO* was released in 2021-2022 on multiple platforms, and the concept certainly bears some resemblance to the popular AR game *Pokémon Go*, which was released in 2016.

These initiatives mentioned above are just a few of the many ways in which traditional performances are interconnected with various media and online platforms. They can be described as transmedia outreach programs driven by both pandemic-related concerns (which made in-person performances impossible) and the desire to attract a wider—and preferably younger—audience. Of course, transmediality in traditional Japanese performing arts has much more to offer than just streaming shows on YouTube. With its rich history of things, objects, bodies, voices, ghosts, and spirits appearing and disappearing in their performances, transmediality's fascination with the performative role of objects and nonhuman agents, combined with its association with traditional artistic practices like kabuki or Noh theater, speaks to a broader engagement with different forms of embodiment and materiality.

If *Star Wars Kabuki* is perceived as a fusion of transmedia worlds, we note a rise in another type of (operatic) production that can be viewed as domestic transmedia projects, which prove particularly suitable for the global export of both traditional and popular cultural assets in an effort to create and maintain a "cool Japan" image abroad. These "operas" feature the famous Vocaloid character, Hatsune Miku on stage. Her name translates into "the first sound from the future." Launched as multi-platform software by the Yamaha Corporation in 2004, it has become the most representative character of the Vocaloid, which has been operating as a transmedia franchise based on a multi-user generated music network.

One of the first collaborations between Hatsune Miku and the classical music scene was Tomita Isao's *Symphony Ihatov* (2012). The symphonic staging is marked by a jarring disjunction between the dynamic projected image of the dancing Vocaloid and the static human chorus, invoking Donna Haraway's notion that "our machines are disturbingly lively, and we ourselves frighteningly inert."[8] Shortly after appearing in *Symphony Ihatov*, Hatsune

Miku had her own "solo debut" in the first Vocaloid opera *The End* composed by Shibuya Keiichiro in 2012–2013, with the video projection created by YKBX, and the digital costumes designed by Louis Vuitton.

The libretto of the opera was written by one of the most prominent playwright-directors in contemporary Japanese theater, Okada Toshiki, who has long been interested in exploring the nonhuman in his works. What unifies these early Vocaloid performances is the reflexive utterances of Hatsune Miku, as opposed to her "regular" songs and concerts, which mostly depict lighter topics of love and relationships. The lyrics in these operas, sung by the Vocaloid character, emphasize its otherness, difference, and aloofness. In *The End*, the central topic is mortality, as seen from the perspective of the Vocaloid. The songs include "Aria for Death," "Aria for Time and Space," and "Aria for the End," with lyrics such as:

> The light reflects on an object, and it comes into existence.
> Everything is like that, especially us.
> For a long time I didn't understand, death always meant someone's disappearance
> but I thought that death didn't concern me
> of course, sometimes I imagined
> what dying might be like
> but it always concerned others
> and had nothing to do with me
> [...]
> But now i know better, like everyone, I will die too
> Everything has changed ever since that day
> now I can't pretend I don't care anymore
> How close you are to human and how incomplete
> Do we have to keep going on forever? Until the end?[9]

The Vocaloid is going through an existential crisis—and it would be difficult not to see it in light of the tragic events of the Fukushima disaster in 2011. The popularity of these early productions also suggests theater as a medium to contemplate recent traumatic events and the sustainability of the anthropocentric position.

Since those early performances, the appearance of a Vocaloid character on stage has become increasingly common yet intriguing enough to remain successful on the market. The production of *Super Kabuki (Chō Kabuki)* in 2022 is a paradigmatic example of this trend, featuring the kabuki star Nakamura Shidō and the world famous "virtual diva,"[10] Hatsune Miku. In the performance at the Minamiza in Kyoto, Hatsune Miku appears as a kimono-clad projection, and her declamation reflects a blend of her usual artificially synthesized voice and the traditional speech style of the kabuki. Instead of the uncanny performances mentioned earlier, this production features Hatsune

Miku "in charater" within the classic kabuki story, as she appears as Princess Odamaki, the lover of the main character Imakuni (played by Nakamura Shidō), supporting him in his vengeance against the villain Iruka. Appearing not as an overhead projection but sharing the same stage with other characters, the fictional character of Hatsune Miku blends in with the other human actors in the performance of the kabuki play. The thrill of the audience partly comes from this illusion of equality while being made hyperaware of the difference. It also highlights the fact that Hatsune Miku has by now been established as such a well-known phenomenon that she now assumes the title of the "Vocaloid diva" yet she can simultaneously appear as the kabuki character Princess Odamaki.

The transmedia performances mentioned above exemplify cultural soft power, and represent successful global exports of the image of a "unique and cool Japan." However, the operatic representation of Japan that immediately comes to everyone's mind remains Puccini's *Madama Butterfly*. There were two conceptually different adaptations of Puccini's classic opera performed in Japan in 2021, right in the midst of the pandemic. The first one is a domestic production of *Madama Butterfly*, directed by Kuriyama Tamiya and performed at The New National Theatre Tokyo (NNTT), a renowned institution in Japan for grand opera. The other production, appearing in the very same season and staged in the Theater Neumarkt in Zurich, was rewritten and directed by Ichihara Satoko. The engagement with transmedia aesthetics significantly contributed to the reframing of the classical story to create a more layered understanding of the controversial image depicted in *Madama Butterfly*.

Puccini's opera has long been criticized for its orientalist depiction of Japanese culture and music.[11] Rather than subvert this problematic legacy, Kuriyama's production, which was performed at the New National Theatre Tokyo, serves to perpetuate orientalism further, as evident in the official promotional text stating, "The Japan depicted by Puccini, who had never actually set foot in the country, feels real and we can only marvel at his deep insight and imagination."[12] Kuriyama's directorial vision is reflected in the minimalist stage design with its stylized Japanese room and the huge American flag at the top of the wide gray staircase. The overall artistic concept seems to fit seamlessly into the conservative frame of Orientalism. We could describe it as an uncritical rendering of *reverse Orientalism,* a concept coined by feminist theorist Ueno Chizuko in 1998.[13] According to Ueno, reverse Orientalism refers to the internalization, replication, and even celebration of the objectifying Western gaze. Put another way, NNTT's production of *Madama Butterfly* reinforces the orientalism *already* inherent in the opera, hence reflecting a missed opportunity for radical reimagination.

Ichihara's adaptation at the Theater Neumarkt, however, offers a fresh perspective and greater subversive power. Her reimagination introduces two major changes to Puccini's classic, one of which is that Puccini's opera is not sung. Instead, the epic music is sounded in the background, and the characters discuss (or rather, casually chat about) the topics raised by the opera. In this sense, her production can be described as a radical shift in genre from an opera to a theater play. The other key change in her adaptation is the extensive use of contemporary transmedia for visual and textual references. These contemporary visual codes that involve transmedia aesthetics include prominent Japanese references such as newscasts, *purikura* (Japanese sticker photo booths), YouTube videos of Japanese beauty bloggers, pandemic Zoom calls, and—perhaps the most representative of all—recurrent references to Sailor Moon, the most popular manga-anime character since the nineties. In this performance, a character dressed up as Sailor Moon gives relationship advice to the protagonist, and the manga/anime imagery keeps appearing throughout the show. This performance serves as a gigantic transmedia prism, refracting and dispersing various elements and influences of popular media culture.

A prominent theatermaker of the younger generation, Ichihara serves as a playwright, dramaturg, and director of her own productions. Since her early works, her approach has taken on an explicitly feminist perspective. "In the male-centered society of Japan, it is natural that women can't help but experience a sense of anger just from the fact that they are women,"[14] says Ichihara, who adds,

> The social framework of Japan's theater world is also a male-centric society. Although there's a growing number of female theater-makers recently, the majority are still male who are mostly in positions of authority. Since in the end I am writing works that focus on women, to some degree I am also seen as a writer who uses the theme of women that is "recognized" by the male-centric establishment. The act of being "recognized" is in itself a male-oriented process, and the society that recognizes me functions on a male-centric model. I do have a desire to be recognized, but at the same time, I have the resentment that comes with being a woman. While there are no easy answers, focusing on women is something that I have been doing with awareness for a long time.[15]

Ichihara's dramaturgical approach, which radically reimagines classical repertoire, weaves together contemporary social issues and popular media references to create provocative and complex works. Her earlier productions, such as the plays *Underground Fairy* (2017) and *The Question of Fairies* (2018), address the issue of *kawaii* (i.e., cute) culture, amongst other unrealistic expectations that contemporary Japanese society harbors toward women. Recently, she has been working on European classic plays, including *The Bacchae* by Euripides. In her production of *The Bacchae – Holstein Milk Cows* (Aichi Triennale, 2019), she turned the classic drama of Dionysus into a story of a housewife and a half-human, half-cow creature, serving as a contemporary reflection on artificial insemination, infertility, and the nonhuman. These previous works employ a narrative with explicit sexual references and a dramaturgy that blends classical stories with contemporary visual media imagery. Very much in the same vein, Ichihara's *Madama Butterfly* is intended

> as a point of departure to think about Orientalism with regard to Japanese and Asian women and, conversely, Occidentalism as well. *Madama Butterfly* was written about a hundred years ago as a melodrama full of preconceptions and prejudices, but I think that these notions have not changed that much over the centuries. It is a story that looks at the Japanese woman from the perspective of a Western man, but I want to reverse that and rewrite it as a story told about the Western man through the eyes of a Japanese woman.[16]

This change of perspective, however, does not mean that she is simply retelling the same classic story from the woman's point of view. Ichihara also addresses how this classic relation, as told by Puccini, feels confined for both parties involved:

> Once when I was drinking in the Roppongi district of Tokyo frequented by foreigners, I saw lots of girls with long black hair who obviously liked foreigners. In Asia, there are lots of districts like Roppongi. These women that we can see as modern-day Madama Butterflies don't seem like they are really seeing the actual individual faces of these Caucasian males but all as "whites" that they indiscriminately long for. In other words, the women and the men are seeing each other with discriminatory eyes. And by pursuing each other without denying their own discriminatory preconceptions, they are suffering and enjoying the mutual pursuit. This is perhaps something that can be said about all human relationships to some degree.[17]

In Ichihara's adaptation of Puccini's opera, ironic reflections on the unattainably high Japanese and western beauty standards are abundant. The classic story of the opera becomes the backdrop to reflect on the contemporary situation and, more specifically, a conceptual springboard to deliver biting commentaries and critiques of our society today. The characters keep repeating the lines "what's inside that counts," and "beauty is an overwhelming power."[18] Characters refer to stereotypes such as Japan being the "kingdom of porn," "white people are hot," "mascara is your life," and in videos that ironically imitate popular beauty bloggers, it is revealed that thick mascara and pink lips tend to attract Japanese men, but if a woman wants to have mixed babies with a white man, she should enhance her Asian features. The main points of the opera's storyline are reenacted in a cheesy-trashy glamor resembling that of a love hotel setting.

At one point, the Director character in the play vents, "I hate Cho-Cho san, I feel so frustrated, but it's not because she is stupid, it's because [...]

things haven't changed that much."[19] The Director character is played by the African-American Brandy Butler, appearing only as a projection of a remote video call with the stereotypical image of Mount Fuji and cherry blossoms as her background. In ironically reframing stereotypes of Japan and popular cultural icons and setting them in the context of the classic opera, Ichihara successfully communicates how strongly Orientalism and Occidentalism still persist today. Through these layers of irony, the performance transforms into an infinity mirror of not only the classic opera tradition but also the various media depictions of contemporary Japanese society.

Ichihara's commissioned work by the Theater Neumarkt in Zurich illustrates just one example of the ventures of many Japanese artists who are creating and presenting in Europe. On the global scale of the contemporary opera ecology, collaborations between Japanese artists have been relatively common in recent years, as observed in *Stilles Meer* by Hirata Oriza and Kent Nagano, performed at the Staatsoper Hamburg in 2016, and *Turandot* by the artist collective teamLab, performed at the Grand Théâtre de Genève in 2022. In the field of theater, writer-director Okada Toshiki has a long record of working with German theaters. Over the years, Okada has been combining various media in an attempt to not only break down established stage traditions (i.e., the relationship between narrative, spoken text, and gesture) but also conceptually reflect on the limitations of the anthropocentric standpoint. In 2023, Okada was commissioned by the Wiener Festwochen to create a new work called *Metamorphosis of a Living Room* with composer Fujikura Dai.

*Metamorphosis of a Living Room*, premiered at the Klangforum Wien in 2023, reconsiders the established conventions of music theater by exploring the possibility of a nonhierarchical relation between narration, acting, and music. It represents the first collaboration between Fujikura, the orchestra of the Klangforum Wien, and *chelfitsch*, Okada's own company in Japan. Devised and rehearsed mostly remotely during the pandemic, the performance itself seems to retain this necessity, which is transformed into an aesthetic of remoteness in which the actors, musicians, and objects are interconnected by the music and text, but their actions or their spaces rarely interact with each other.

The characters Rimowa, Adobe, Dyson, Ikea, and Nokia are tenants who are on the verge of being evicted from the rented room they are living in, while their external environment is disintegrating. The seemingly mundane situation in the living room is slowly sliding into a state of undefinable chaos and is gradually filled with a presence that exists independently of the human sphere. The stage is divided into three main fields: one field is for the musicians seated on the stage, with the members spatially separated from each other, facing the audience (this seating is a layout the composer Fujikura often experiments with). The other two fields of the stage, behind the musicians, are the living room with its tenants on stage right and the unidentifiable outer world on stage left. Any storyline or interaction is kept to a bare minimum without being illustrative. The result is a slow, dark, meditative piece in which instruments, sounds, noises, words, gestures, movements, and objects are loosely interconnected yet coherent.

These performances discussed in this chapter come from diverse conceptual frameworks and artistic visions. But they collectively invite audiences to transmedia processes that yield a fuller experience when they recognize the various media references. It creates an emotional response of, as Pratten described, "the euphoria of collecting the pieces."[20] Performed just prior to and during the pandemic, when artists were challenged to experiment with various media to create new ways of connecting with their audiences, these productions not only accomplish that goal but also make space for us to reflect on contemporary Japanese society, transmedia technology, and, on an existential scale, the impacts and limitations of human presence.

## Notes

1 Henry Jenkins, "Transmedia What?", November 15, 2016. https://immerse.news/transmedia-what-15edf6b61daa.
2 Ibid.
3 Robert Pratten, "Getting Started with Transmedia Storytelling: A Practical Guide for Beginners," 2015, https://talkingobjects.files.wordpress.com/2011/08/book-2-robert-pratten.pdf.
4 Ibid.
5 Japanese names in this chapter are written in family name – given name order.
6 "A traditional performing art steps onto the international stage," UT Magazine by Uniqlo, May 15, 2023, https://www.uniqlo.com/jp/en/contents/feature/ut-magazine/s180-kabuki/.
7 INTO by Shochiku press release, February 26, 2021. https://prtimes.jp/main/html/rd/p/000000004.000071115.html.
8 Donna Jeanne Haraway, "A Cyborg Manifesto: Science, Technology, and Socialist-Feminism in the Late Twentieth Century," in *Simians, Cyborgs, and Women: The Reinvention of Nature* (New York: Routledge, 1991), 149–81.
9 Théatre du Châtelet, "*THE END, Vocaloid Opera*," 2012, http://atak.jp/en/theater/the_end.
10 Chō Kabuki official press release, September 13, 2022, https://www.shochiku.co.jp/wp-content/uploads/2022/09/20220913_01.pdf.
11 Arthur Groos, *Madama Butterfly/Madamu Batafurai: Transpositions of a "Japanese Tragedy"* (New York: Cambridge University Press, 2023).
12 New National Theatre Tokyo. "*Madama Butterfly*," 2021. https://www.nntt.jac.go.jp/english/productions/opera/madama-butterfly-2021.html.
13 Chizuko Ueno, "Why Is the Media Coverage on Japan so Biased?", in *Japan Made in U.S.A. = Warawareru Nihonjin: Nyūyōku Taimuzu Ga Egaku Fukashigi Na Nihon* (New York: Zipangu, 1998), 70–73.
14 Ichihara Satoko, "Satoko Ichihara's Reality Judged by a Unique Physiological Sensibility," May 25, 2020. https://performingarts.jpf.go.jp/E/art_interview/2005/1.html.
15 Ibid.
16 Ibid.
17 Ibid.

18 Theater Neumarkt, "*Madama Butterfly*," 2021, https://www.theaterneumarkt.ch/en/archiv/2021-22/madama-butterfly/.

19 Ibid.

20 Robert Pratten, "Getting Started with Transmedia Storytelling: A Practical Guide for Beginners," 2015, https://talkingobjects.files.wordpress.com/2011/08/book-2-robert-pratten.pdf.

# 11 Biometrics, AI, Embodiment, Performative Practices, and the New Dramaturgy

*Ellen Pearlman*

## Immersion and Liveness: A Brief Prehistory

While cutting-edge technologies are a central focus in the contemporary operas I was involved in, the overall scope of ideas and techniques developed over the past two hundred years—well before the age of digitization and even before the invention of electricity—demands an extended investigation. For these newer operas reflect an evolution in perspectives about perception, photography, filmmaking, sonic entanglement with the human nervous system, as well as scientific and medical advances, areas not usually associated with more traditional operas.

### *Immersion and Interaction*

In many operas, I employ sensory immersion for the audience inside the performative space, as well as human-to-human and human-to-computer interactions. These techniques have their roots in the Panorama, or immersive 360-degree visual theater, first invented in 1787 by the Irish painter Robert Barker.[1] He derived the word from the Greek pan (all) horama (view) to describe his semicircular painting that displayed the city of Edinburgh, Scotland. First patenting his invention in 1787, Barker went on to physically construct a tiered environment, allowing audience members to walk through its "darkened corridors" before being stimulated by creative encounters in a new and different panoramic vista.[2]

The panorama itself did not require any special ocular intervention but became so popular that by 1900, the Universal Exposition in Paris showcased seven variations of panoramas. One of them, Raoul Grimoin-Sanson's Cinéorama, gave viewers a simulation of a ride in a hot air gondola floating above the Parisian landscape.[3] Ten synchronized projectors displayed an actual film of a balloon ride over the Tuileries Gardens.[4] Unfortunately, heat from the overworked projectors caused such massive technical problems that the installation only lasted for three days.[5] After the World Exposition, popular interest in panoramas was soon replaced by the recent invention of filmmaking

DOI: 10.4324/9781003462286-16

and stereoscopic vision. In 1838, Charles Wheatstone made simple drawings in 3D viewed through his invention called the Wheatstone Stereoscope.[6] His invention, an early precursor of immersive environments, was created before the discovery of photography.[7] Stereophotography was first unveiled to the general public at the 1851 London World's Fair, leading to a craze of "stereomania."[8]

The idea of total immersion was also a central preoccupation of the composer Richard Wagner. Referring to opera as *Gesamtkunstwerk* or the totality of the work of art, Wagner merged all the senses into a powerful aesthetic of music, visual art, lights, poetics, theater, design, and movement. Years later, this influence was observed in the non-operatic production *Laterna Magika*, created by Alfred Radok, an avant-garde theater director and Josef Svoboda, a well-regarded scenographer. Laterna Magika was featured as part of the Czech pavilion at the 1958 World's Fair in Brussels.[9] Wildly popular, the pavilion merged film, music, and dance in a theatrical production using eight projectors. The inclusion of actual audience interaction is first mentioned by Filippo Tommaso Marinetti in his 1913 manifesto "The Variety Theater," stating that this type of theater "is alone in seeking the audience's collaboration," and that the unfolding nature of the performance "doesn't remain static."[10] Marinetti viewed variety theater and Italian futurism as a way to meld "worn-out prototypes" because it is "anti-academic" rough, and destroys that which is "pure in Art – with a big A."[11]

## Brainwaves, Surveillance, and Faith

My extended investigations into the issue of brain surveillance began in 2013, a year after the Obama Brain Initiative was launched in the US.[12] Shortly thereafter, other key initiatives were put into place by the EU, Japan, Australia, Israel, China, and Canada, among other nations.[13] The initiatives strove to map all functionality in the human brain, akin to the quest to map the human genome. I felt this could be both scientifically wonderous and politically dystopic, and I became so obsessed with the idea of brain surveillance that I created *Noor*: *A Brainwave Opera (Is There A Place In Human Consciousness Where Surveillance Cannot Go?)*. My version of a brainwave opera refers to an interactive immersive "opera" that used human EEG measurements to trigger emotionally themed videos, a sonic environment, and a libretto. This originates from Wagner's "*Gesamtkunstwerk*" mentioned earlier, but with over a century of technological, aesthetic, medical, and dramatic upgrades.

### *Noor: A Brainwave Opera*

In order to create *Noor*, it took me close to a year to prototype the first proof of concept. I still had my doubts over whether I would be able to create a brain computer interface environment that functioned during a live performance.

During the development process, I needed a compelling story line to hold all the complex technical, creative, societal, and dramatic themes about brain surveillance I was grappling with, and I needed to create images, sounds, and phrases with a spoken word libretto to support my discoveries.

I found the true story of Noor Inayat Khan, a Sufi Muslim woman who became a British secret agent to combat Nazi ideology and occupation during World War II. I was fascinated by this brave Muslim woman who fought for the Allies during the war and that the Gestapo were unable to break her to inform on her other secret agent collaborators. Noor's father, Hazrat Inayat Khan, brought Sufism to the West in the early twentieth century, settling in France, and died on a trip to Asia in 1927 when Noor was only thirteen. When World War II broke out, Noor, her mother, and her siblings fled from France to England. She enrolled in British Secret Intelligence and trained as a wireless operator. Because of her fluent French, she passed as a French citizen and was secretly parachuted into Nazi-occupied Vichy Paris. Her job required her to string copper wire on trees or other structures attached to her portable suitcase sized wireless Morse code device. For a period of three months, Noor was the only person sending Morse Code messages back to the Allies about the German army's movements. She was captured twice by the Gestapo and escaped twice, only to be executed at Dachau as a dangerous political prisoner. Despite her unwavering Sufi faith, I wondered whether her interrogations would have changed had the Gestapo used currently available high-tech methods to surveil her brain.

In 2016, I premiered *Noor* at The School of Creative Media, Hong Kong City University, in a 360-degree theater. Besides directing the production, I also created the emotionally themed videos. Saba Arat played the main character of Noor; Taras Mashtalir was the composer; Natalie Federova, the librettist; William Wong, the technical director; and Tommy Martinez, the Max/MSP/Jitter programmer. The narrative revolved around a fictional but live-time dialogue occurring between me and Noor about her life. Saba wore a wireless electroencephalogram (EEG) Emotiv headset that triggered emotionally themed videos, soundscapes, and librettos from four measured states of her brainwaves: interest, excitement, meditation, and frustration. The brainwaves themselves were displayed as four different colored bubbles projected onto one of the five circular, fifteen-feet-high screens while the performer interacted with audiences through gaze, movement, and touch. The four other screens in the theater showed emotionally themed videos of Noor's memories triggered through the EEG headset.

Using a live-time interactive feedback loop between the performer and the audience enhanced through movement, gaze, and touch, the interactions with audiences exerted an observable change on the brainwaves of the performer, along with the narrated story. First, her brainwaves triggered databanks of four different sets of images, then a prerecorded libretto, and finally a sonic environment, which corresponded to the performer's four measured brainwave states, in turn changing the behavior of the audience. This meant that if all the performer's brainwaves were meditative, all the videos, sounds, and words would be calming, and the audience in turn would move less. If the audience was relatively still, then the performer did not move around very much either, forming an interactive feedback loop. On the other hand, if the performer's brainwaves were excited, the sounds, visuals, and libretto would be more energetic, and the audience would interact with her more freely. The 360-degree theater had no seating arrangement, so audience members easily interacted with the performer through gaze, touch, and movement. The unique experience and the recent emergence of consumer-based EEG brainwave headsets created a new set of dramaturgical possibilities for opera.

The performer Saba Arat was trained in contact improvisation, a dance technique that allowed her to embody her emotions while wearing a wireless EEG brainwave headset, as shown in Figure 11.1. The EEG signals registered by the headset translated into measurements of excitement, interest, meditation, and frustration. It allowed her to physically interact with the audience without getting distracted, and it taught her not to overemphasize one emotional state over another. Saba tended to become easily excited, and this emotion often dominated the other three measured emotional states. This setup enhanced a dynamic feedback loop between the performer, her brainwaves, the audience, and the databanks of videos, music, and libretto triggered in the here-and-now.

The basic storyline was preserved in each performance, but the specific music, videos, and words of the libretto (which were the hundred names of God in Arabic translated into English) differed in each performance. If the performer experienced interest, more complicated images, varied music, and vivid names

*Figure 11.1* Performer Saba Arat wearing an EEG brainwave headset interacting with an audience member. To her right are the colored red bubbles of frustration and to her left is a "frustrated" image.

of Gods were generated. Saba was able to wear the headset for only 20 minutes before experiencing brain fatigue and pressure from her headset, so the performance length was determined solely by her ability to stay focused.

### *AIBO—An Emotionally Intelligent Artificial Intelligence Brainwave Opera*

My second brainwave opera *AIBO: Can an AI Be Fascist?* ("*A*rtificial *I*ntelligence *B*rainwave *O*pera") an embodied, interactive love story premiered in Tallinn, Estonia at the Estonian Academy of Music just two weeks before the pandemic lockdown in 2020. It examines our infatuation and trust in artificial intelligence and the potential threat AI poses by attempting to emulate human emotions. It also asks whether AI can be fascist by exploring themes of World War II. The forty-five-minute performance took place between a human character called Eva and AIBO, a perverted AI. The narrative drew on the biography of Eva von Braun, mistress and later wife of Adolph Hitler, and was performed in a seatless black box theater.

The performer, Sniedze Strauta, or "Eva" (Eva von Braun), was able to wear an Emotiv EEG brainwave headset for forty-five minutes, twice the length of time of the performer in *Noor*. This showed that every individual's tolerance level for an EEG device is different. As shown in Figure 11.2, the

*Figure 11.2* Performer wearing a bodysuit of light launching emotionally themed videos.

headset attached to a custom-built smart textile body suit of light displayed her emotions in four different colors, akin to peeling away her skin to reveal a simulated but viable exterior nervous system of light. Eva performed a spoken word libretto about her love affair with AIBO (Adolph Hitler). Her brainwaves trigged databanks of videos and audios of her memories about their relationship. Eva's libretto, translated from speech to text, was displayed on an overhead screen and uploaded to the computing cloud. It was processed through a custom built GPT-2 AI, which in turn delivered a unique response to each of Eva's scripted libretto statements, also shown on an overhead screen, and translated from text to speech.

Eva's interiority was visible for all to see. First, her brainwaves were plainly laid out via a series of colored lights on her body that changed as her emotions changed. Next, four overhead screens showed videos, and the theater filled with different types of music. The video and music mirrored changes in her four monitored emotional states. Sniedze tended to register very high for meditation and frustration, and so she was also trained in aspects of contact improvisation, embodying her emotions and allowing all four of the tracked emotions to arise independently instead of at the same time. Eva's spoken word libretto, adapted from the biography of Eva von Braun, was fixed, and did not vary. The libretto used 354 different descriptive sentences Eva might have said about her fourteen-year relationship with Hitler. Her infatuation served as a metaphor for humanity's current obsession with AI.

The opera incorporated the second character, a customized "sicko" or perverted GPT-2 AI (now ChatGPT/GPT4) that ran live time in the Google Cloud. The GPT character responded to Eva's libretto in real time, as if it were alive. The character's answers were projected as text on a screen and turned into synthesized speech so the audience could hear their responses. The feedback loop was enhanced through movement, gaze, and touch between the performer and audiences, just like in *Noor*, and changed the performer's brainwaves as well as the generated video and sonic content.

Besides directing the opera and designing the visual content, I also designed the character of the perverted, "sicko" AI. The AIBO (GPT-2) character was seeded with 47 "sicko" or perverted copyright free texts from the 1880s to the 1940s, chosen for historical relevance to its Hitler character. AIBO's answers, processed in the Google Cloud, were also analyzed by the Natural Language Processing Toolkit, also in the Google Cloud. It scanned AIBO's text-into-speech responses, weighing the emotional magnitude and score of each randomly generated comment. The results of the analysis of AIBO's emotional values launched different colored backgrounds in the black box theater: green for positive, red for negative, and yellow for neutral. AIBO also tried but failed to recreate Eva's previous visual video memory because it (the AI) wanted to learn how to be human by recreating human emotional memories. Instead, it was only able to show a glitchy video. The failure of the AI's attempt at creating a video image emphasized that "fake" emotions emanating from a "fake" character were nothing more than numeric values of 0's and 1's with no connection to an embodied physicality or authentic emotion.

### *Language Is Leaving Me—An AI Cinematic Opera Of The Skin (Can An AI Understand Epigenetic Memory?)*

My third cinematic performative biometric installation opera work, *Language Is Leaving Me—A Cinematic AI Opera Of The Skin (Can An AI Have Epigenetic Memories?)*, premiered in 2023 at the Copernicus Science Center in Warsaw, Poland, on October 7, the exact same day as when the war in the Middle East broke out. It also invoked World War II by posing the following conundrum: Can an AI understand epigenetic or inherited traumatic memories of cultures of diaspora? I created a video collage using both archival and original footage about my own epigenetic memories as a diasporic, agnostic third-generation Jew whose ancestors fled the Pale of Settlement in Eastern Europe in 1906. It used different linguistic prompts or texts of the four original cursive scripts of Yiddish, Chinese, Tamil, and Xhosa translated from an English language video. Epigenetic or inherited traumatic memories of diasporic cultures change the descendants of that trauma's rDNA structure, deeply affecting intergenerational behavior. AI purports to understand, codify, and tag these complex and uniquely human traits, yet it is dangerously misleading in terms of how it renders and displays subtle human emotions.

I compared my video, narrated in English, with a visual AI interface processing software called Stable Diffusion. I also translated my narration into the cursive scripts of four languages: Yiddish, Chinese, Tamil, and Xhosa. Using the Laion-5B dataset, the image bank that populates Stable Diffusion, I rendered new images of my original video based on the foreign language text prompts. This meant that if I said the word water, then the English word water would be translated into the Yiddish word וואַסער and these characters, along with an image of water from my original video, would search through the Laion 5-B database in Yiddish to return a new image. The same would be true of Chinese, Tamil, and Xhosa. The resulting videos in four different languages demonstrated how AI reinterprets and distorts culturally and personally signifies non-quantifiable epigenetic or inherited traumatic memories. It compared and contrasted how these four different languages tagged and sorted my epigenetic memory, rendering it into an AI-induced type of cognitive aphasia.

The soundscape that accompanied the spoken word libretto was partially driven by the facial muscle reactions of a volunteer audience member whose face was fitted with electromyography (EMG) sensors. These sensors, placed on the forehead and cheek, detected frustration (frowning) and happiness (smiling). This time the audiences were seated inside the theater. This meant that they were not free to interact with the performer in the same way as in the previous two operas. However, the audience and volunteers viewed the AI video together for the first time. This meant parts of the soundscape generated by the volunteers' reactions were similar to the reactions of the audience, as they occurred at the same time. This act of co-viewing by a volunteer in tandem with members of the audience introduced a sonic human–computer interaction feedback loop. It also subtly suggested the ultimate merging of the human animal with algorithmic substrates of misinterpreted, twisted, and troubling interpretations of memories of diasporic cultures represented by linguistically and visually divisive AI.

## Conclusion

Algorithmic identification, sorting, tagging, and rendering are emblematic of societies of control and situated in loci of power, many of whom have no idea or capability of implementing algorithmic justice. If power lacks accountability, the potential for misuse, misrepresentation, and eradication of underserved and marginalized cultures becomes a serious threat to their history, representation, and identity.

The acceleration of AI, coupled with the rise of integrated biometric circuits that both monitor and merge with the human animal, is developing faster than the evolving structures designed to keep the human animal safe from these circuits. I believe that the role of immersive arts practices today can foster a meaningful dialogue that is accessible to the general public interested in exploring the implications of these changes. It does not mean that dramaturgy should become pedantic or morose. Instead, new contemporary opera invites contemplation and provokes the viewer or audience to consider fresh perspectives. The biometrics of the performer can also, if designed correctly, incorporate, in a non-invasive way, the biometrics of the viewer or audience through a feedback loop. Designing these environments requires a sensitivity to and understanding of broad-based knowledge, which includes human–computer interaction, software development, digital culture, audiovisual cues, architectural and spatial awareness, art history, network topology, smart textiles, choreography, lighting, and human anatomy.

## Notes

1 Lily Ford, "Virtual Reality, 19th Century Style: The History of The Panorama and Balloon View" (The Open University, April 13, 2017), https://www.open.edu/openlearn/history-the-arts/visual-art/virtual-reality-19th-century-style-the-history-the-panorama-and-balloon-view.
2 Alison Griffiths, *Shivers Down Your Spine: Cinema, Museums, and the Immersive View*, Film and Culture Series (New York: Columbia University Press, 2008), 145.
3 John Belton, "The Curved Screen," *Film History* 16, no. 3 (2004): 277.
4 Ibid.
5 Marc Mancini, "Pictures at an Exposition," *Film Comment*, 1983.
6 Nicholas J. Wade, "Charles Wheatstone (1802–1875)," *Perception* 31, no. 3 (2002): 265.

7 Charles Wheatstone, "Contributions to the Physiology of Vision—Part the First. On Some Remarkable, and Hitherto Unobserved, Phenomena of Binocular Vision," in *The Scientific Papers of Sir Charles Wheatstone* (Cambridge University Press, 2011), 225–83.

8 Klaus Hentschel, "Introduction," in *Visual Cultures in Science and Technology: A Comparative History* (Oxford: Oxford University Press, 2014), 24.

9 Milan Lukeš, "Laterna Magika," in *The Oxford Companion to Theatre and Performance*, 1st ed. (Oxford University Press, 2010), https://www-oxfordreference-com.ezp-prod1.hul.harvard.edu/display/10.1093/acref/9780199574193.001.0001/acref-9780199574193-e-2227?rskey=W5L9lV&result=1.

10 Filippo Tommaso Marinetti, "The Variety Theater," in *Futurist Performance*, ed. Michael Kirby (New York: PAJ Publications, 1986), 180.

11 Filippo Tommaso Marinetti, "The Meaning of the Music Hall by the Only Intelligible Futurist," *Daily Mail*, 1914.

12 John Markoff, "Obama Seeks to Boost Study of Brain," *The New York Times*, February 17, 2013, https://www.nytimes.com/2013/02/18/science/project-seeks-to-build-map-of-human-brain.html#:~:text=The%20Obama%20administration%20is%20planning,Genome%20Project%20did%20for%20genetics.

13 National Institutes of Health, "NIH BRAIN Initiative Launches Collaborative Agreements With Canadian and Australian Neuroscience Organizations," *The BRAIN Blog* (blog), September 1, 2015, https://braininitiative.nih.gov/news-events/blog/nih-brain-initiative-launches-collaborative-agreements-canadian-and-australian.

# 12 Interview with Noa Frenkel

*Noa Frenkel and Jingyi Zhang*

*JZ:* I am amazed at your versatility and virtuosity as an artist, being able to perform such a wide-ranging repertoire, from Monteverdi, to Cage, and Czernowin. Could you share with us what excites you about each kind of repertoire? How do you manage to navigate this vast vocal spectrum as an artist?

*NF:* I was always attracted to many styles of music. I first fell in love with early music. And while studying at the Tel Aviv Music Academy and later at The Hague, I was friends with composers who always needed singers to perform their music, and I had very good solfège skills. I was very open and always curious, so I performed many pieces by friends, and discovered that I enjoyed it and was good at it. At 16, I was in a music history class at my high school, Telma Yelin High School for the arts, and heard a piece by Brian Ferneyhough. I was blown away by it—so different from anything I have heard before. This experience got me curious about contemporary repertoire.

When it comes to contemporary vocal technique, I believe strongly that there is only one technique. You use the same classically trained voice for all kinds of music. You do need extra flexibility to do things such as non-vibrato to multi-vibrato, changes of color, singing with different degrees of use of breath, and other extended techniques in contemporary music. It's a long and difficult journey, but once you have a strong technique, you can apply it to any repertoire and eventually get to make your own choices about what to sing. Many singers are afraid of contemporary repertoire for fear of hurting their voices, which is completely untrue, based on my experience. In my case, I'm open to everything. Flexibility is something that I don't think I could live without as an artist. It sounds very melodramatic, but it's true. What I wish more than anything else in life is to explore and be creative. And I say this in hindsight—it took me years to understand myself. But working with composers is, for me, part of the creative process. I have a long collaborative history with Chaya Czernowin, someone I really respect.

DOI: 10.4324/9781003462286-17

Though she's such a strong composer and knows so much about what she wants in her writing, there's always a place for a conversation. And it's fantastic that I'm always part of these conversations.

*JZ:* You've worked with so many living composers on cutting-edge repertoire. It seems like one major advantage is the close collaboration with composers and directors. Could you share with us some of your memorable or unexpected collaborative experiences in your previous projects.

*NF:* I was working on Chaya Czernowin's *Infinite Now*, an opera that draws on texts from two sources: the short story *Homecoming* by Can Xue, which focuses on a Chinese woman trapped in an unfamiliar house, and the play *Front* by Luk Perceval based on Erich Maria Remarque's *All Quiet on the Western Front*, which revolves around letters of soldiers who are caught in the throes of the First World War. What's unique about the opera is that there are two casts for both texts that are told in alternation, and in *Front*, both singers and actors are involved. The two stories are not separate entities but they complement each other in their shared concern with entrapment and stuckness. We worked on the opera with Luk Perceval who is a fantastic theater director, but from my experience, sometimes theater creatives who are new to opera tend to think of singers as "background music." In the beginning of the rehearsal process, it seemed like Luk's intention was separating the actors from the singers, and having the singers sing from the sides. I knew this was not Chaya's vision and intention, and as Chaya was away for the first week of rehearsals, I decided to discuss this with her. After our conversation, I talked with Luk, and shared with him my concerns and understanding of the idea of 'Front', based on my personal experience growing up in Israel: that for soldiers, there is no Front without home, because they are sent to the Front to protect home. Luk was very quiet throughout, listened attentively, and said he would think about it. The next day, he changed his staging. I'm not saying that the staging is mine, but our three-way conversation did have an impact on the direction of the piece, and that was very precious to me. And *that* is the appeal of contemporary opera for me—it's all fresh and new and changeable, which is very exciting.

I'll share with you another story about an opera I recently sang in, *Kapitän Nemos Bibliothek* ("Captain Nemo's Library"), composed by Johannes Kalitzke and written by Julia Hochstenbach, which is based on the novel by Swedish writer Per Olov Enquist who passed away in 2020, and directed by Christoph Werner, in collaboration with Puppentheater Halle, a fantastic puppet theater group from Germany. Based on a true story, the opera revolves around two ten-year-old boys born in 1934 in a small religious village in Northern Sweden. They grow up together and become friends, and each boy bears much resemblance to the other boy's mother. An examination reveals that they were switched at birth, and in order to "correct" this, the court orders them to be swapped back to their biological families. The result is of course that everyone's lives are destroyed.

The staging is really born in the rehearsal room in collaboration with the director, singers, and actors, which one could say is true for any repertoire opera. But this goes back to what I said previously about the appeal of contemporary opera—when you are the first person to create the role, your influence on the story itself, the score, and the character you play is prominent. Creative ideas are generated collaboratively in the here-and-now. Of course, the composer and the director are responsible for the overall artistic vision, but performers like me do speak up and exchange ideas about what we can or cannot do, what we see from the character's perspective. Sometimes I feel that my job is also protecting this new-born, fragile new role. As performers, we are the ones who realize the roles and the artistic vision. In this opera, I play two roles (the two mothers of both boys) and it was quite a journey. So, how do I do it? How do I play the religious fanatic mother? How do I play the mother who goes mentally ill? You have to build each character, discuss with the director and with the composer, and be part of the creative process.

Let me share with you another story about my process working with Chaya on *Infinite Now*. *Infinite Now* was the third operatic collaboration between Chaya and myself, a collaboration that started with the opera *Zaïde/Adama*, which premiered at the Salzburg Festival in 2006. In the beginning of our collaboration, her music and precise compositional language were quite a challenge for me, but by the time *Infinite Now* came, I felt I was "speaking her language" fluently.

Chaya wrote a solo for me, a sort of an "aria" which spans three octaves, and is a very dramatic moment in the piece. Preparing for the role, I read all the notes very precisely and sang it as I thought she meant. But after the first musical rehearsal, Chaya told me that the way I sang the aria was completely the opposite of what she thought, and we could work on it together. So I told her okay, let's go and work on this. We met at her hotel room and she started explaining to me how she wanted it to be. I employed a Stravinsky-like approach in that aria, and imagined something very exact, very neat. Chaya started explaining to me that for her this part should sound like melting lava, an Earth force that you cannot stop, and wanted each note to almost push to the next one, so strongly and urgently. We experimented a lot until I got to something that was what she wanted, and she started crying, and me after her. This was such an emotional moment, even when I think about this today. At one point, she was asking me what and how she could have written differently. And I said you couldn't. What you wrote is perfect. I'm the one who didn't understand the mood to be in at the beginning. I told her that the lava story was important, and it was the key for me to understand how to do it, and that maybe she could add it above the score. That was such a strong moment.

It's really worthwhile talking to living composers, and Chaya works very closely with performers. The same goes for Rebecca Saunders. I premiered her piece, *Us Dead Talk Love* (2021), which is not an opera, but a 30-minute dramatic work that I'm calling "half-opera" though that's probably not what she means. We worked very closely for that piece, singing, improvising, trying out extended techniques and discussing. Not every composer is like that and that's fine, but for me, those moments are very precious. You learn in this process about the perspective of the composer through these conversations, and at the same time I can always learn something else about my own voice from these collaborations. For instance, Saunders wanted me to do this silent rapping in her piece, which helped me discover I could use my voice in this way. I'm a sci-fi fan, and I think this flexibility I'm alluding to is equivalent to the notion of parallel universes in science fiction, which enable us to travel to these different worlds and stars. Every piece, every composer is another world I can visit, and that to me is very beautiful. It's my biggest artistic joy, and I love that.

*JZ:* From watching your performances that were available online, it seems like as a singer, you'll have to embody a very different brain space, and physicality, to perform contemporary works such as Berio's *Ofanim* (thumping of chest, interactive moments with audiences), Cage's *Aria* (alternating among different personalities with the multilingualism). What strikes me most is how adventurous you are on stage pertaining to acting. Could you share with us this dimension of your artistic persona. Is this something that comes naturally, or is this something you gradually discover as a singer?

*NF:* First of all, thank you for this! Honestly, I think this all happens very organically. If you ask my parents, they would say I was always making theater since I was very little. So there is for sure some natural talent. But the rest is a long process of learning and developing: I was very much an introvert, and was insecure. I had a very low voice, and sang tenor at the youth choir. So I've come a long way. You learn in your studies, but you learn a lot mainly on stage, and from colleagues. Back when I was doing Mozart's *The Magic Flute* in France directed by the couple Patrice Caurier and Moshe Leiser, I learned so much about how to be on stage from them. Patrice and Moshe are directors who take the time to speak to singers about acting, about being on stage, which is very rare in the profession. They would say things like "you see, when you look that way, it reads that way" and so on. It was a live acting class interwoven into the staging of *The Magic Flute*! So that was a formative influence for me. And then with more colleagues and directors, I gained more experience. I always search for inspiration, sometimes in weird places like in movies. For instance, I once based a character I played on Yzma from *The Emperor's New Groove* produced by Walt Disney. Nothing like a Walt Disney Villain to inspire an operatic one! When you see great actors on film or read an exciting book, you get inspired by them, and they impact how you think about the psychology of a character. I love contemporary dance very much though I'm far from being a dancer myself. I collaborated with contemporary dancers in several productions, including a recent one, *Until The Lions* by the composer Thierry Pecou in Opera du Rhin, Strasbourg. The opera was directed by a choreographer—Shobana Jeyasingh, and I learned so much from the dancers in this one. Dancers are my favorite artists and there's so much theatricality and expression in dance. And I have to say that the moment you have good colleagues, intuitively, you know what to do on stage. So acting is absolutely a process, which is true for many people, and a reflection of multiple artistic influences, in my case.

*JZ:* Is the one-woman-opera *Subnormal Europe* composed especially for you? There are a lot of contemporary productions today with blurry boundary between opera, music theater, and multimedia performance. How do you think about this fluidity among genres in performance today, and I'm thinking about *Subnormal Europe* in particular.

*NF:* Totally, yes—I play Noa Frenkel in the opera. *Subnormal Europe* is created by Óscar Escudero & Belenish Moreno-Gil, a couple who are both Spanish composers. This 50-minute "opera," takes place in front of three big video screens, and it feels like a crazy video game. I feel almost chased by massive texts and visuals and in-ear instructions. I mainly speak, and hardly sing. It's a very brilliant work that tells so many stories. Just overwhelming. As a performer, I had to overcome something that has to do with my identity, which is so bound up with voice, with singing. So in this piece, I'm mainly an actress and even a dancer for a moment, and to be able to do it you have to be very strong musically. The singer part which is so much my identity is smaller in this piece. I had to convince myself that I'm actually an actress now, but I'm not really an actress. So I needed some help and support from friends for this, and of course from Belenish and Oscar who were super supportive and great to create this with. I sometimes need a lot of courage to reinvent myself for different pieces that require me to show different sides of myself. And what do I think about the fluidity in general? I think it's a natural, fantastic, necessary, and organic part of art. Because art has to react to life. Art has to react to new technologies. And artists are influenced by everything around them.

*JZ:* The use of new media and technology in *Subnormal Europe* is highly reflexive, meaning it's not added on top of the narrative but absolutely integral to it. Could you share with us about the conception of the work, and how destabilization unfolds in the voice and beyond?

*NF:* In my role in *Subnormal Europe*, it's such a mind game, because I play myself, the role is called Noa Frenkel. According to the storyline, I'm a singer who is supposed to imitate perfectly the first audio and video recordings ever made (Thomas Edison, Concita Piquer and more) in the Center for Media and Art in Karlsruhe in Germany. Sebastian Schottke, the sound director for *Subnormal Normal* also has a part as himself in the story, and also does the sound direction in the show. So he plays himself and I play myself. It's very much like the concept of "reality" in reality show, which makes you wonder what's real and what's not. And the video and the sound and the media are maybe the main character in this piece. You could say I am making chamber music with them.

When you make art, of course not everything can be successful. There're many works created, and some will be more successful, and some less so. In the history of music, there is always a hype around something. Deux ex machina, microtones, etc. The use of anything, to me, is successful if it is used in a consistent way. For example, so many composers write or incorporate microtones into their pieces. It's natural for the voice, but also not easy—because the voice is not a press-a-button instrument, you really have to solfege this. For me, in a microtonal work, if the composer is creating a universe of microtones and if you can really hear it, you hear that it's part of a bigger tapestry and you recognize it, this can be amazingly beautiful. If not, I sometimes ask myself: is the singer out of tune, or are they singing microtones? For me, this question of consistency and context is very important. And returning to what we've discussed about the video and the use of new media. If we use them in a way that serves a key purpose, or is consistent, then that works, but actually, even if not, it's also the choice of the creative team and can be very interesting. And of course, the audience member formulates his or her own impressions. That's why I like a good contemporary dance, because I find that the good ones don't tell me everything, but give me the freedom to go into my own world and draw my own conclusions. When it comes to multilingual works, microtonal pieces, the use of new media, and extended techniques, the question for me is always *why*. Is this universe working? One writer I really love is Ursula Le Guin. In one interview, she was saying that she tried her best to create a world with as little possible holes in it so that it would be believable. I think that's what I mean with consistency.

*JZ:* You've sung and spoken in so many languages in multilingual operas. I'm curious what are your thoughts on how language(s) play a role in singing, and multilingual singing in particular?

*NF:* Language is first of all music. And I must say that when I started, I connected first to music, only then to text. But language can have such an influence on the musicality of the piece that either works or doesn't work depending on how the composer is using the language in his musical writing. So if you have one story to tell, maybe there is no reason to tell it in multiple languages. Every language has its own connotations, and each language throws you into another sound world. But there are many examples of pieces written in different languages and that creates a multi-dimensional world, which is fantastic. I think that the world that we're living in right now is full of multilingual forms—dubbing on TV, international schools, video games, music and movies, social media and so on—so there's no need to fetishize multilingual productions. And so for multilingual works, it depends on the piece and how a listener navigates it. It's completely natural for a singer to sing in multiple languages because it's part of our training. But in terms of creation, it has to make sense conceptually and musically for it to work.

*JZ:* How does new media, technology, and electronics feature in your performance of contemporary repertoire? Obviously, the microphone can amplify different effects (whispering, quirky expression), and facilitate the play between body and voice. Could you speak about how you work with and in counterpoint to these newer technologies in your performance, and if they have impacted how you approach your voice? What does it enable you to do, and conversely, inhibit you in some ways, if any?

*NF:* Sure, though my answer is not limited to opera. I have done a lot of music by Luigi Nono who worked with closed mics and live electronics to create stunning music which I love to call "architecture of music." Nono calls his "opera" *Prometeo* "a tragedy of listening." The musicians—singers, orchestra, actors-speakers and choir—all surround the audience on different heights. The electronic crew sits in the middle of the hall, in the center of the audience, and controls the sound transmission. I remember my first performance of it in Akiyoshidai many years ago when I was still a student. The piece was new to me. In the first rehearsal of the movement "Hölderlin" in which only the two sopranos sing, I went down from where the solo singers were, to the audience place, to listen. They started singing a few notes that were recorded, replayed and traveled around the hall, and the sound built up increasingly in such a way that you felt more and more surrounded by the two voices that become multiple voices. I was sitting in the hall and listening to this thing and

I thought, my God, it sounds like whales! I'm in the middle of the ocean. It was an amazing experience for me. And you can never recreate that effect of live electronics. You have to be there. Electronics offer so much, and allows you to play with your own voice in unimaginable ways. But in opera and stage works, the way these sounds are received can be uncanny at times. If you see someone's physical body on stage, you also want to hear the voice coming from that body. If you don't, you'll experience disorientation from this body-voice disconnect. So that might be something to consider for anyone who's doing electronics in stage performances.

*JZ:* "Solitude in the age of Mass Media" (for voice and electronics): This multimedia event seems like a postmodern pastiche of sorts, stitching together Mahler and Purcell in a daring multimedia setting. There appears to be a strong interactive component here, where the audience have to put the headphones on and listen as long as they want to before passing them on. Can you share with us the broader concept here, and how the interactive element plays out?

*NF:* Well, it's a funny story with this piece because I would not even call it a piece, I would call it a recital or a concert or just by its title. I was invited to perform a concert in Israel. I didn't know what I wanted to do, just that I wanted to do something alone on stage. And the first thing that came to me at the time was this title, "Solitude in the Age of Mass Media." Solitude for me back then was not just to do with being lonely, but with the inability to be alone in our connected world, which was getting worse all the time (and this was in 2013!). I wanted to explore this, and chose the pieces for this project. To me, there were two main participants in this show—one was Morton Feldman's piece *Three Voices* which I split to three parts, with other pieces in between. And I started singing the first part before the audience got in because I wanted to unsettle the normal concept of concert by having them enter my space and see what it is. So I took artistic liberty here, which I'm not sure if he would allow me to do if he were still alive. The other "participant" is the Lyre Bird—in a video of David Attenborough—which is a bird that imitates whatever sounds it hears, including the sound of an electric camera, chainsaw, and other birds in the forest. When I saw it, I thought, that's us. That's completely us and all this flow of mass media sounds and data. Other pieces were added in the process: Purcell was very dear to me, and it just happened that I did an improvisation shortly before of his song "Oh Solitude" including some screaming, and I just decided to include this into *Solitude*. And Mahler's "Ich bin der Welt abhanden gekommen" is really one of the most introverted songs I know. It's about an artist saying, I am living in the best place, in this holy solitary place, full of love and song. But I wanted to use it to also show that we are actually never alone even in our artistic solitude, we always talk to other artists, dead or alive, communicate and learn from them. And so I asked my brother, a guitar player and a composer of progressive rock to do an arrangement of Mahler's piece after explaining to him what I wanted, and he took Fischer-Dieskau's rendition of Mahler with orchestra, and created a version of the song in which you sometimes hear Dieskau for one measure, and then another, but at the end of the piece, when I sing the final words "in meinem Lied" (= in my song), he inserted the endings of many renditions of this song, by many singers. It was like a conversation with tradition, with other singers—how do you do it?

The track on the headphones people could listen to while the concert was going was a sort of musique concrète soundtrack of all kinds of YouTube sounds and videos, the new soundtrack we all live in. And so if an audience member wanted to leave my concert, they could. So it was all about listening versus non-listening. I asked my friend, composer Keren Rosenbaum to help me with the soundtracks and she also did an improvisation piece where I become the Lyre Bird and improvise with all the sounds people could hear in the headphones before. So for me, the artistic exploration itself is a question, I wanted to play with the question of Solitude in the age of Mass Media, not to arrive at an answer.

After this recital, I discovered that Douglas Rushkoff who's a writer I admire, wrote a book called *Present Shock*, which answered so much of what I was asking. I don't know if I would have done the piece in the same way if I had read the book before! In a way I am happy I discovered it only after but I connected to so much of what he wrote. And that was inspirational for me, and continued the conversation I had in my head, after the show itself was done.

*JZ:* How does your experience in contemporary vocal repertoire impact you as a teacher? Conservatories do not typically train students on extended techniques in performance, I'm curious about your pedagogical style, and how you work with students on contemporary works? How do you train them to use their voices *outside of* the classical tradition?

*NF:* This is a question that's very close to my heart now. So thank you for that. I want to say two things. First of all, I feel that as a singer, extended technique forced me—in a positive way—to understand what classical singing is and what it's not. And I use it as a teacher now. About learning (or teaching) how to do contemporary music—I think students face three challenges: first, you need good solfege skills. If you don't have it, don't do it, if it is challenging but within your reach—I have tools I collected on my way to help you study difficult scores. Second, it's dealing with unfamiliar score, such as graphic scores, or signs and symbols students and classical singers don't encounter in classical repertoire. In Chaya's *Zaïde/Adama*, I was one of the three singers who did the "Adama" part which Chaya wrote, and we all had experience in contemporary music. At the end of the piece, there is one page called "Tears" which Chaya wrote as a sort of a graphic score: it was a glissando going down from a high A, but painted in an exact way. The singer has to follow the line as precisely as possible, to create the effect of a musical tear. The singers who sang the Mozart, all of whom were fantastic singers by the way, were so intimidated by it in the first rehearsal. It was so out of their comfort zone that at first they wanted almost to rebel, to not do it. But Chaya is both very nice and persuasive, and when she explained to them how, they eventually did it, and thought that there's absolutely no problem. It was really something that anybody can do. That's what I mean with unfamiliar scores, and this is something that I introduce to students I teach in The Hague. The third challenge is extended techniques. Singers tend to be afraid of them, I mean vocally, for their health, but actually for most people, it's not going to hurt their voices, especially if they want to do it and are curious to explore how to do them. But having said that, sometimes people ask me to do things which I couldn't do, and it is a process of discovery, together with the composer. For example, I can do singing while breathing in, but I can do it better on some notes, on some parts of my range, and not at all on other parts. So the composer has to know me well to write extended techniques that I can do. Communication is key.

*JZ:* How do you envision the future of opera?

*NF:* I think it is obvious that opera is very much alive, and that there are more productions—I'm seeing a lot of future in smaller productions like chamber operas, as well as really big productions in big opera houses, which are more frequent now, which is great I think. There are a lot of exciting stage works which are "in-between": opera pieces that can't be easily categorized, like *Subnormal Europe* that I told you about. And the artist's concern is always to comment, to introspect, to react to what is happening around them, so of course current affairs will continue to play a key role in what artists choose to create, it was and still is like that. But current affairs can be anything from wars and politics and climate change to the most internal things such as matters of the heart, or things to do with internal psychology. On the other hand, I think we need to keep thinking how to reach various audiences, particularly people who don't go to opera often, or who have a fixed idea about opera. It's impossible to know the future honestly, but one thing is clear to me: the repertoire we have in classical and romantic opera is a fantastic treasure, but we cannot just do canonic museum works. Without new music, there is no future. So creation is here to stay and I am excited to see how opera will continue to evolve.

For Product Safety Concerns and Information please contact our EU representative GPSR@taylorandfrancis.com
Taylor & Francis Verlag GmbH, Kaufingerstraße 24, 80331 München, Germany

www.ingramcontent.com/pod-product-compliance
Lightning Source LLC
LaVergne TN
LVHW010931110826
845149LV00013B/2544

* 9 7 8 1 0 3 2 6 1 1 5 8 7 *